Praise for *In The Beginning Were the Women*

"Claire McKeever-Burgett reminds us that women have always been at the heart of the biblical story, even when denied the chance to speak for themselves. Their stories are crucial in helping shape our understanding of truth, justice, and love. This book is all at once restorative, empowering, and visionary. And it invites us as readers and people of faith to honor scripture, reclaim what has been silenced, and embrace our shared humanity."

— Malynda Hale, Actress, Activist, Executive Director of The New Evangelicals

"In Jewish tradition, we speak of the Tanakh / the Hebrew Scriptures as black fire on white fire. The black fire is the letters on the parchment; the white fire is the fertile blank space that surrounds them. *In the Beginning Were the Women* is white fire. These imagined voices of our Biblical mothers light the way to new understandings. From a Hagar who speaks her truths of slavery and gives a name to the Holy One to a Huldah who knows that God is an action (and that action is Love), these are women of integrity, wisdom, and courage. Meeting them in these pages inspires me to return to these sacred stories anew. And like the midrashists of my tradition, McKeever-Burgett knows that no one interpretation is "the right one." We find God in the many-splendored multiplicity of our imaginings. This is how we are made in the Image and the Likeness: our words create worlds. I thank God for the worlds within these pages."

— Rabbi Rachel Barenblat, author of *70 faces: Torah poems and Texts to the Holy*

"This is storytelling at its best! Based in scripture, drawing on history, and filled with imagination, Claire McKeever-Burgett offers not only creative stories, but liturgies, prayers, music and reflection questions to guide her readers into everyday life. I wish I'd had In the Beginning Were the Women in seminary!"

— Rev. Jane Vennard, Spiritual Director, Author of *Fully Awake and Truly Alive: Spiritual Practices to Nurture Your Soul*

"At a time when women's rights are under threat and Christian nationalism is on the rise, Claire McKeever-Burgett's *In the Beginning Were the Women* offers a refreshing and necessary voice. Unflinching and unapologetic, yet tender, this book makes space where there has long been constraint. McKeever-Burgett invites us into expansiveness, into a vision of women's stories and wisdom too often minimized or erased. Wherever you fall on the spectrum of religion or gender, this book challenges you to think big about the ways women have molded, shaped, and created movements. It is both timely and timeless, and it deserves to be read widely.

— Raena Boston, Writer, Advocate, and Co-founder Emerita of the Chamber of Mothers

"Reading *In the Beginning Were the Women* made me fall in love with Scripture, God, and the complexities of my own life. Rather than simply telling us *about* the women of the Hebrew Bible, Claire draws us into their story and invites us to find our place in it. It's a kind of odyssey into the dynamics of our own lives. One does not merely read this book, one is transported *by* it. All I can say is that I want more: more of Claire's writing and more of the wisdom and strength that she gives us all."

— Rev. Dr. Maria Kane, Rector, St. Paul's Episcopal Church, Waldorf, MD

"As a pastor and preacher, I often wrestle with how to capture the depth, humanity, and complexity of the women in the Hebrew Bible. Once again, McKeever-Burgett has offered a profound gift—one that enriches both my theology and my ministry. She finds a way to weave scriptural imagination, theological insight, and deep reverence for the ancient women of our faith. Her creative storytelling and the interactive aspects of each chapter allow me to really engage in the text with mind, body, and spirit. My congregation loved her first book; I have no doubt they'll embrace this one just as wholeheartedly. McKeever-Burgett continues to shine a light on stories too often overlooked, misinterpreted, or forgotten—and we are better for it.

— Rev. Margie Quinn, Vine Street Christian Church

"Claire McKeever-Burgett has been one of my greatest teachers in learning to listen to and follow women's wisdom. With *In the Beginning Were the Women,* Claire brings that gift to readers by giving voice to the women of the Hebrew Bible with honesty, poetic imagination, and deep spiritual insight. Moreover, she provides prayers, liturgies, and practices to help those women's stories inform our lives today. This book belongs in the hands of anyone longing for a more just, whole, and life-giving faith."

— Johnny Sears, Executive Director, Upper Room Programs & Director, The Academy for Spiritual Formation

"Claire McKeever-Burgett, through the vignettes and stories contained in *In the Beginning Were the Women*, gives a gift to woman-folk everywhere (*and to those who love them*). Through Claire's eyes we are enabled to *see* women once rendered invisible by sleight of pen. Through her ears, we have an opportunity to eavesdrop and to contemplate their choices and ours in the poetic and comforting language of woman-speak. Through liturgy, poetry and song, we celebrate forgotten and overlooked women. Through the structure of this book, we are invited to *assume* a role in the ongoing biblical narrative. Are we Matriarch, Mystic, Wise Woman, Warrior, or some combination of all four? *In the Beginning Were the Women* is not a book for tourists or spectators. Claire calls us to dwell, to wade in deeper waters with these Old Testament women as we contemplate the messy business of living faithfully in unfaithful times."

— Safiyah Fosua, retired associate professor of preaching, Black and Womanist Theology, Christian worship and Christian ministry, United Methodist clergy

"Claire McKeever-Burgett has gifted us a rich remix of sacred stories, pungent in their power to make us notice the divine feminine in Scripture again for the first time. Accessible enough for the uninitiated yet in-depth enough for the seasoned, her work beckons us to believe the women who began it all.

— Dawn Darwin Weaks, pastor and coauthor of *Holy Disruption: A Manifesto for the Future of Faith Communities*

"Reading *In the Beginning Were the Women* felt like being invited into a circle of sisters, mothers, and ancestors who affirm that I have always carried wisdom in my bones. Claire McKeever-Burgett retells women's stories from scripture, allowing them to breathe new life into each of our lives. Her words remind us that women's voices are not accessories to God's story; they *are* the story. With poetry, liturgy, and sacred imagination, Claire calls us to remember the divine feminine within us and around us, to trust our own bodies and voices, and to believe that liberation is the heart of God for everyone. I will draw from this book over and over again in my own individual and communal spiritual practices."

— Chelsea Kim Long, writer, meditation teacher, neighborhood pastor, spiritual guide,and author of forthcoming book on imagining Christianity outside of the patriarchy from Westminster John Knox

"My concurrent roles as pastor, parent, and professor often feel impossible to hold together. *In the Beginning Were the Women* manages to speak to each of the audiences I juggle and their sometimes competing needs. McKeever-Burgett has brought together responsible Biblical study, liturgical and spiritual creativity, and gorgeous prose to reveal and remind us that the complicated realities of womanhood and mothering have always been a part of the story of God's people. We owe it to the women who have gone before, to ourselves, and to the creation still unfolding, to cherish these stories and be inspired to share our own."

— Rev. Blair Trygstad Stowe, Assistant Professor at Claremont School of Theology and Co-Host of The Progressive Christians Podcast

Praise for
Blessed Are the Women

"Praise the Great Mother for the birth of this book! For the creativity, honesty, beauty, and labor of its author, Claire McKeever-Burgett. This book is for all humans who long to sit in the lap of the Holy One and to be nurtured in love and story. Blessed are the women who went before us and who walk with us even now. And blessed is this beautiful creation."

— Rev. Beth A. Richardson, writer, artist, storyteller, and liturgy nerd; Dean Emeritus of The Upper Room Chapel

"Claire McKeever-Burgett has captured the process of midrash in her book and skillfully relates her *midrashic* accounts to the experiences women have had throughout time. She brings to life women in the Christian Scriptures, some named there and others nameless until McKeever-Burgett gives them names and identities. By including her own experience throughout the work, she makes women's stories real as she teaches truth."

— Rabbi Emeritus David Horowitz, Temple Israel Akron, Ohio and Past President, PFLAG NATIONAL

"In *Blessed Are the Women*, Claire McKeever-Burgett lifts up the deep well of women from which we come, and through these women, she offers us audacious vulnerability, expansive liberation, powerful witness, and creative contemplative connection so that we can more fully be healed as we remember–love holds us still."

— Rev. Molly Brummett Wudel, Co-Pastor of Emmaus Way, Durham, North Carolina

"*Blessed are the Women* is a liberating guidebook for a deeper and wider relationship with God through scripture. Rooted in the author's lived experience, it opens needed space for so many of our stories. The words within its pages show us what it can look like for women to take up space in the story of God."

— Rev. Molly Vetter, Senior Pastor, Westwood United Methodist Church in Los Angeles

"*Blessed Are the Women* is not a story only for women. It's a story for all of us who yearn to embrace the fullness of God's goodness within us and to live and love with the fullness of our enfleshed selves. *Blessed Are the Women*/Claire is a trinity of gentle wisdom, tender mercy, and inexplicable beauty that I will be sharing with colleagues, friends, and parishioners. To know Claire and her work is to know what wisdom, tenderness, brilliance, and grace look like in human flesh."

— The Rev. Maria A. Kane, Ph.D., Rector, St. Paul's Episcopal Church, Waldorf, Maryland

"*Blessed Are the Women* gives voice to the actual daily lives of biblical women. Each woman is visited in her own world, and speaks words of healing and wholeness into our world. These words are given theological depth through original music and liturgy. The music is beautiful (and singable!), the liturgical resources theologically elegant, and the suggestions for action and ethical witness at the end of each chapter open the reader's eyes to new possibilities for changing the world in which we live. I strongly recommend this book for preachers, liturgists, teachers, and small group leaders."

— John S. McClure, Charles G. Finney Emeritus Professor of Preaching and Worship Vanderbilt Divinity School

"This extraordinary book integrates the stories of biblical women, with profound contemporary experiences of women's bodies and sexuality, in ways that are stunning, healing, invitational, and prophetic. The recommended reading, viewing and listening resources and the reflection guide make it accessible and ready to use for individuals or small groups. I can't wait to introduce *Blessed Are the Women* to others, and to use it as a resource for healing retreats and groups for women."

— Elaine A. Heath, Ph.D., Author of *Healing the Wounds of Sexual Abuse: Reading the Bible with Survivors*, and co-author of *Trauma Informed Evangelism: Cultivating Communities of Wounded Healers*

"*Blessed Are the Women* invites us to meet and remember Jesus through the lives of women coping with oppressive social and religious realities. Just as our faith journey relies on creative imagination, so does our ability to engage the depths of their stories. They are named. They have traumatic histories. They are strong and courageous. They have much to teach us. This creative rendering of their stories guides our Christian discipleship."

— Luther E. Smith, Jr., Professor Emeritus of Church and Community, Candler School of Theology, Emory University

"Savor this book! *Blessed are the Women* is a tender gift for hungry souls and neglected bodies longing to find gospel companions bearing honest witness to the wonder and frailty of life. Claire's determination to unapologetically proclaim all the news — good, conflicted, life-giving, and incomplete — she's heard from the mothers of the Jesus story and wise women she's met along her own journey will inspire and challenge you."

— Rev. Amos J. Disasa, Senior Pastor, First Presbyterian Church of Dallas

"Claire McKeever-Burgett takes women seriously. Because of that, this book feels both wizened and somehow brand new; ambitious yet matter-of-fact. *Blessed are the Women* was a delightful read."

— Shannon K. Evans, author of *The Mystics Would Like a Word* and *Feminist Prayers for My Daughter*

"For those who long for imagination, long for women's voices to not simply be included but to be celebrated and centered in their faith practice, Claire has written this for you. She has written it for us. Blessed are the women, indeed."

— Jenny Booth Potter, author of *Doing Nothing is No Longer an Option: One Woman's Journey Into Everyday Antiracism*

"This book is premised on the notion that we can expect to hear God's Word anew when we show up to Scripture. Claire is helpfully pointing back to a range of stories (women's stories!) through which we can discover ourselves (and God) again and again. The associated prayers, liturgies, and music enable us to move past a static reading of these narratives and to start living into them, as these women's experiences have the potential to reorient and characterize our lives today. In that sense, it is a gift."

— The Rev. Zachary Thomas Settle, PhD; Editor-in-Chief, *The Other Journal*

"*Blessed Are the Women* is appropriately named, but don't let the title confuse you. This is a book that men need to read also. Given the patriarchal history of American Christianity, we men need to understand how we have been complicit in harming women and how we can be transformed by listening to their wisdom and following their lead. As McKeever-Burgett writes, "Without women we don't have Jesus. We don't have Christianity. We don't have any of it." Christian men would do well to sit with the truth of that statement and reading the stories within this book could enable that truth to sink deep into their souls."

— Rev. Dr. Christopher Carter, Associate Professor of Theology at Methodist Theological School in Ohio, and Lead Pastor of The Loft at Westwood United Methodist Church in Los Angeles

"McKeever-Burgett holds a profoundly incarnational theology, integrating spiritual reflection with practical embodiment. Hers is an original voice, forged in the crucible of her own pain, fear, and grief, tempered by courageous self-examination, intuitive vision, and poetic joy. *Blessed Are the Women* is holistic, designed to foster communities who read, reflect, worship, and share stories together, empowering one another for the sake of healing, freedom, and justice. These pages contain a forceful rebuke of patriarchy and an open invitation to move toward sacred, life-giving wholeness for all."

— Marjorie J. Thompson, author of *Family: The Forming Center* and *Soul Feast: An Invitation to the Christian Spiritual Life*

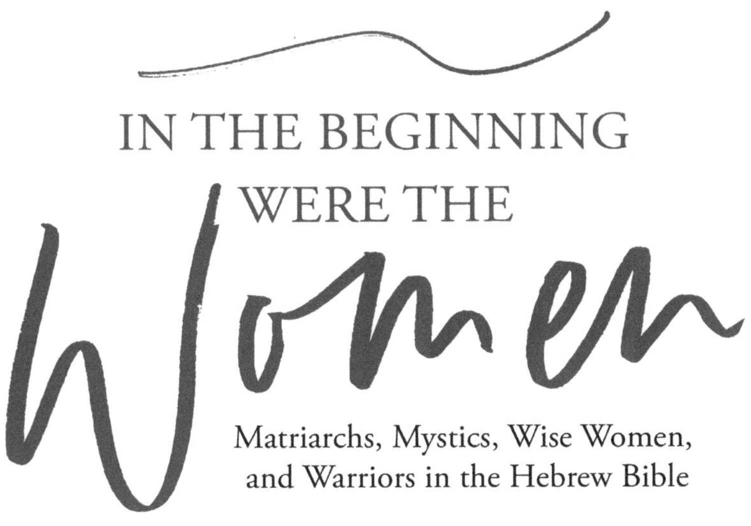

IN THE BEGINNING WERE THE Women

Matriarchs, Mystics, Wise Women, and Warriors in the Hebrew Bible

CLAIRE K. McKEEVER-BURGETT

Except where noted otherwise, the Bible translation used throughout is the New Revised Standard Version Updated Edition (NRSVUE).

Print: 9780827216853

EPUB: 9780827216860

EPDF: 9780827216877

ChalicePress.com

For every woman whose name we do not yet know and whose story we have not yet heard,
and for every woman whose story has only been told by men:
this one's for you.

Contents

Introduction

I wrote *In the Beginning Were the Women* in the summer and fall of 2024 when bombs rained down on Palestine and Lebanon, destroying lands and loved ones. Any possibility of ceasefire became a distant and forgotten dream. I wrote this book when the first Black and South Asian American woman ran for the office of President of the United States, offering many of us hope that the equity and justice we'd been fighting for as women all these years was not lost. At that time, I was caring for my aging parents and young children, longing for the days when we lived in small villages of no more than one hundred souls and when resources and time were shared; and it didn't take an hour, a full tank of gas, and untold texts and emails to get the kids to school, soccer practice, and friends' houses, and my dad to medical appointments.

I wrote the manuscript while sitting in my recliner, driving in my car, lying in my bed, and walking in the neighborhood. I wrote it at kickboxing classes as I pondered ancient women doing the same—kicking the air, punching their imaginary opponents, sweating, strengthening, fighting. I wrote it in the mountain desert of Utah, and by the Tennessee River. I wrote it in the shelter of an oak tree and under the bright noonday sun, on soccer field sidelines, at the voting booth, and in the kitchen. I wrote it like a prayer, asking God and the women for help every step of the way because writing, like life, is best done together.

In many ways this book was much harder to write than *Blessed Are the Women: Naming and Reclaiming Women's Stories from the Gospels*. First, because as a Christian I'm much more familiar with the women of the synoptic gospels than I am with the women of the Hebrew Bible.[1] Second, because the Hebrew Bible mentions more women

[1] The Hebrew Bible (often called the Tanakh in Jewish communities) is a collection of the sacred writings of Judaism, which include the Law (Torah), Prophets, and Writings. It is important that the study of the Hebrew Bible and the women within it stand on their own, apart from the New Testament, because the stories in it were originally told long before Jesus entered the scene. It's also important to allow its stories to stand apart from the New Testament to avoid

than does the New Testament, though many of those women remain unnamed and underrepresented. In one study of the Hebrew Bible, I found a total of 1,426 names, of which 1,315 of referred to men and only 111 to women. Seventy percent of the named *and* unnamed women in the Bible come from the Hebrew Bible.[2]

Studying the women of the Hebrew Bible was a time-consuming endeavor, as was choosing the women about whom I wanted to write. I also listened deeply to who wanted me to write about them. Because I wrote this book like a prayer, I wasn't the only one doing the choosing. Rather, it felt like a communal effort between God, me, and a host of women calling out from both the page and the space between the pages for their sacred stories to be told.

Another challenge was refusing to transpose Jesus into the stories of the Hebrew Bible. My professors at Vanderbilt Divinity School had been the first to teach me that the Hebrew Bible stands on its own, without the New Testament, and that it is important to read and study in and of itself, rather than as a precursor to the stories of Jesus and the formation of the Christian church.

To study the Hebrew Scriptures without the lens of Christianity is not easy, especially when you've been taught for years at church that Isaiah is prophesying about Jesus as the Messiah and that Jesus is a direct descendant of Rahab. However, it's not that I don't read certain texts, like Hannah's prayer, and understand immediately where Mary gets inspiration for her own song in Luke. Rather, as I read Hannah's prayer and then bring background, context, and story to it; I write, read, and tell it in a way that enables it to stand on its own without the overlay of Christianity, because that's how it was

---

supersessionism, the idea that the Christian church superseded Judaism and the Jewish people and that the New Covenant through Jesus Christ supersedes the Mosaic covenant. While Christianity and Judaism share similar origins, they are distinct faiths with different religious texts. Though Christianity recognizes the Hebrew Bible as part of its scriptural canon, Judaism does not recognize the Christian New Testament, and instead of this being problematic to me as a Christian feminist theologian and storyteller, it is respected and celebrated both within the pages of this book and in the whole of my life.

[2] Toni Craven; Ross Kraemer; Carol L. Myers, eds., *Women in Scripture: A Dictionary of Named and Unnamed Women in the Hebrew Bible, the Apocryphal/ Deuterocanonical Books and New Testament* (Boston: Houghton Mifflin, 200) xii.

originally prayed. The rabbis compiling the stories were not doing so from a Christian viewpoint—and neither should I.

Make no mistake, I'm a professing Christian and a follower of Jesus and of the women whom he followed.[3] So I'm mindful about offering worship and presenting stories about the women centered in the Hebrew Bible. And I understand their stories not in light of Jesus or Christianity, but in light of God's loving nature, God who bestows redemption, forgiveness, and reconciliation as gracious gifts to us and through us. The Hebrew Bible tells the story of God, *and* it tells the story of God's people. It asks, "Who is God?" as well as "Who are we?"

We humans have been asking these questions of God and ourselves since the beginning of time. In many ways, the scripture texts we have about God and God's people offer us an epic, and often exhausting, love story. It is a back-and-forth saga, in which God is clear about what is required to live a loving, peaceful, just, and merciful life, and in which we humans become confused about our faith and embodying it in our lives.

One point of confusion is about the role of women in the stories of faith. There is confusion, primarily, because women did not get to tell their own narratives. Instead, society assigned the "headier" matters of translation and storykeeping to the male scribes and rabbis.[4] Therefore, the relatively few texts that we do have about mothers, mystics, wise women, and warriors in the Hebrew Bible are incomplete, told from someone else's voice, perspective, and with someone else's agenda.

What might be different about Deborah's song if heard from her feminist point of view? How might Hannah's prayer be fully

---

[3] If you're confused by this statement, wondering, *Who were the women Jesus followed?* read my first book, *Blessed Are the Women: Naming and Reclaiming Women's Stories from the Gospels*.

[4] Though Judaism has existed for thousands of years, women have only been allowed to be rabbis in the United States for the past fifty or so years. Sally Priesand was the first American woman rabbi, ordained on June 3, 1972. However, Rabbi Regina Jonas was the very first woman rabbi, ordained in 1935 in Germany. Her ordination thesis was "Can a Woman Be a Rabbi According to Halachic Sources?" Rabbi Jonas was deported to Theresienstadt during World War II, where she worked side by side with Viktor Frankl, meeting the trains of Jews from liquidated ghettos to help with mental health and to provide crisis intervention. She was killed at Auschwitz in 1944.

understood in the context of birth as a means of survival? What is the Witch of Endor's name? Is Woman Wisdom in Proverbs 31 concerned with being an obedient and model wife, or might she have a different message and interpretation of her life and its purpose?

I'm hardly the first to ask these questions or the first to retell women's stories from the Bible, and I pray I'm not the last. I join a long line of feminist storytellers and theologians[5] reclaiming and naming women's stories everywhere, and I come alongside womanist theologians and storytellers[6] who've been telling us for centuries that many of the lesser named and lesser glorified women of the Bible are the true warriors of justice and love.

In the spirit of the lesser-named and lesser-known women from the Hebrew Bible, the stories I tell within these pages center and celebrate them. For example, Aholibamah, the scandalized mother, Bilhah and Zilpah, the forgotten mothers, and the prophet Huldah, the Woman of Thebez, and the warrior woman, Jael. Many of these women are not actually Hebrew women; rather, they are the (often) enslaved people from the lands that the ancient Israelites conquered (or tried to conquer).

They are the marginalized, the oppressed, the ostracized, the "other." They are also the brave, the saviors, the leaders, and the lovers offering us a mirror to see ourselves more clearly. While I'm a socially constructed white woman who is doing the ongoing work of

---

[5] Feminism is the belief that women should have the same political, social, and economic rights as men. Feminist theology and storytelling, then, is a movement calling for the reinterpretation and reexamination of religious and spiritual traditions, practices, and scriptures through a feminist perspective. It challenges male bias in religion and society and seeks to create more just and egalitarian communities for and with everyone, though it has, throughout its practice, often left Black women and other Women of Color out of its scholarship and perspective, which, through engaging my ongoing antiracism work, I seek to correct in my own life and work.

[6] Womanist theology is a theological approach that centers the experiences of Black women, particularly African American women, in its analysis. It offers a critical response to other liberation theologies, such as Black Liberation Theology and certain feminist theologies, which it considers limited in scope. Womanist theology rejects the idea of redemptive suffering and instead identifies oppression as the result of unjust systems and focuses on themes of liberation, survival, and hope. I'm a student of both feminist and womanist theology, which I hope is evident in how I tell the stories in this book.

excavating white supremacy[7] and patriarchy[8] from my very bones, I try to tell women's stories with as much awareness as possible, given my social circumstances and experiences.

However, dear reader, when you read the stories of these women and you find yourself wishing their stories were different in some small or big way, when you find a story that feels incomplete, or—gift upon gift—when you find ones that inspire and uplift, still; tell the stories in your own words: Expand them. Make them better. The graciousness and mystery of God is that the story does not end with one person's period, nor does it begin with only one person's word.

Even now, as I write the opening pages to this book, I hope one of you women reading this introduction will pen a story about Eve or the Witch of Endor or Miriam and her mother. We need thousands of stories from thousands of women about the women of our faith, for without them we'd have very little faith at all. Our imaginations are a gift from God, an inherent part of our being as humans. To expand our hearts, minds, and bodies beyond the pages before us and into the pages we can imagine can be an act of faith, spirituality, and prayer. It can even be an act of worship, the work of the people of God, together, imagining and reimagining stories that center those traditionally pushed to the margins; the work that celebrates those whom God loves—everyone.

The hope and the prayer is that women's stories continue onward, in and through us—flowing like rivers, rocking like oceans, simmering like fires, expanding like air, grounding like dirt—so that we can continually experience and know the truth and its merciful unfolding.

Though I've organized the chapters and stories of this book into four sections—Matriarchs, Mystics, Wise Women, and Warriors—any of them could fit into any section. Mothers are warriors, wise

---

[7] White supremacy maintains that white people are superior to people of other races, and therefore should dominate them. White supremacy as a political ideology imposes and perpetuates cultural, social, political, historical, and institutional domination by white people.

[8] Patriarchy is a social system that assumes that men are superior to women and that both men and women have specific roles they are to play, and therefore rules they must follow. Hence, when men, women, queer people, etc. differentiate from the norms of patriarchy and break patriarchal rules, they face additional challenges, oppression, inequity, violence, and more. All systems based on domination and control lead to violence and inequity.

women are mothers, mystics are wise, and warriors are mystics. As you read, I offer definitions of *matriarchs, mystics, wise women, and warriors* at the beginning of each section, and, as you'll see, their definitions overlap in many glorious, synchronistic ways.

Moreover, by using feminist theological interpretation, I found that I'm better able to contend with the more violent and war-drenched texts. While I did not erase death, domination, and murder from the stories, I did try to understand the motivations for self-defense and protection from a woman's perspective. When the story is told from Jael's point of view, for instance, we gain greater insight into why she might be motivated to kill a king for reasons other than protecting the man to whom she is married or helping the Israelites gain political control.

I do not wish to justify murder or war; I also do not seek to judge it or the women in these stories. Rather, I hope to offer a way into the more violent narratives that invites nuance, curiosity, and kindness. Might it be part of our spiritual practice to suspend judgment, and, instead, practice openness and wonder? Might it be part of our faith formation to open wide our arms to the women who were forced (and still today are forced) into ways of living that they might not have chosen had they had other options? How might we, as people of faith, seek not to be understood but to understand, not to be loved, but to love?[9] My hope is that you'll feel the interconnectedness of the women and their myriad roles throughout the stories of this book, gaining a deeper vision of women's complex, layered, and multidimensional lives—way back then, as well as today.

Like *Blessed Are the Women*, I wrote this book to be useful—to preachers, teachers, parents, professors, grandmothers, mothers, liturgists, and worship leaders, to name a few. Within the pages of this book are detailed backstories, feminist renderings of traditional scripture passages, and visions of women circling up to heal, love, and protect. There are grandmothers and aunties, husbands and sons, kings and queens, daughters and sisters. There are searing critiques of patriarchy and gracious offerings of God's love for all.

---

[9] From the prayer attributed to St. Francis of Assisi, first published almost seven hundred years after his death; I imagine St. Clare (Francis' devotee) praying it alongside the women, who needed its words in a world that often silenced them.

Each chapter introduces you to a story of a woman from the Hebrew Bible, a liturgy for personal or communal use, questions for reflection, and contemporary connections to both music and woman-led nonprofits doing the work of love and justice today, because what good are our prayers on Sunday if they hold no meaning in our lives on Monday?

I am a preacher at heart, and stories and ideas come to life for me through the spoken word. Hence, the women's stories may read like sermons because, as I wrote them, I also spoke them aloud. I imagined what each story would sound like and feel like if shared from a pulpit—how the narrative would land in a community's collective heart, how a woman's name and life might teach and transform, and how a rhythm and a cadence might carry a message straight to the core. It was imperative that the women's stories read well on the page, as well as preach well with others. After all, their stories are embodied through and through. What the women say is *always* connected to the bodies from which they speak.

Additionally, the liturgies in each chapter include a song of praise that I wrote as I was driving home one cold December day, meditating on God and the women. Like Hannah and Miriam, I couldn't help but sing in response to God's presence, light, and love, so I (safely) located the voice recording application on my phone to capture the sacred tune that was rising within me. Later, with the help of my dear friend, Beth Richardson, we transcribed the tune so that you and others can sing it too.[10]

Singing, after all, is the language of the divine feminine.[11] The low hum of breath in labor, the melody that spills forth when we circle up and share our stories, the groans too deep for words, the prayers we can only pray when we sing them. So, sing beloveds, and when you do, know that you sing with Mother God and the women themselves, whose melodies keep us alive.

Following the Song of Praise in each chapter's liturgy is a Contemporary Connection section, in which I share modern-day song

---

[10] You can hear me sing it, acapella, at clairemckeeverburgett.com/music.

[11] The divine feminine spirit is not limited to one gender or identity and represents qualities of intuition, creativity, emotional intelligence, compassion, nurture, empathy, and connection that can live and grow within all of us.

suggestions for you to listen to as a part of your worship. After all, our worship is not meant to be divorced from our everyday lives but is, instead, intended to transform and accompany them, revealing to us that the Holy is everywhere and in everything, even and especially in the music we may not traditionally associate with "church." I have chosen different songs for each chapter and liturgy according to the themes present in the story. Perhaps these modern melodies will inspire you to dance, sing, and play as a part of your daily spiritual practice and not separate from it.

To close each liturgy, *The Prayer of the Women* serves as the common prayer, inviting us to imagine the words of women's prayers to and with Mother God throughout time.

When I was eighteen and a first-year college student, an older classmate and friend said to me over coffee one morning, "You know God's not male right?" Instead of refuting this truth, I leaned in and said, "Oh thank God! Tell me more." Thus began the conscious work and practice of understanding God as God and not as he/him/father/male. It's been twenty-five years since then, and I'm still doing the work to excavate patriarchal constructs of God from my very bones. Patriarchy is deeply steeped in our culture, in our religious and spiritual practices, and in the oxygen we breathe that it takes conscious, intentional, and daily effort to remove it from our imaginations. It takes deliberation and focus, time and sacred energy to imagine something new, and there's no work I'd rather be doing.

Hence, I refer to God as *Holy Mother* and *Mother God* (sometimes *Mama God*) throughout this book. I truly believe that if women had written these stories and liturgies, they would have prayed to a Mothering God and not a Fathering one, though both can teach us beautiful things about the God who ultimately defies all categories, genders, and human constructs. In these pages, though, I imagine ancient women in need (as I am, too) of a soft-bosomed, woman-like, mother-like God who holds us in her loving arms in and through all of life's complexity, heartbreak, and beauty.

Finally, I understand *woman* more as a verb than as a noun. To *woman* is to live in such a way that uproots and uplifts the untold, incomplete stories of our lives and places, at the very center, the voices and the names of those whom society, culture, and systems have relegated to the sidelines, or tried to erase altogether. In this way, one's body does not make them a woman as much as one's life and how they live it does. However, our bodies *do* matter because of the ways women's bodies have been hypersexualized and shamed (especially when those bodies are of the conquered and colonized people) while men's bodies are, by and large, unexamined and lifted as the standard bearers for all. Therefore, placing women, our bodies, and the stories we hold within them at the very center of our sacred narratives is an essential practice for the reclamation of our faith in God and of God's faith in us.

In a conversation with Gloria Steinem at The New School in October 2014, bell hooks said, "Patriarchy has no gender, and I think we have to remember people's allegiance to patriarchy isn't static. People can start out in feminism and end up in patriarchy.[12]"

Hence, when I pray things like, "Women forever and ever amen," I mean women and men and nonbinary people who follow the divine feminine spirit of justice, love, and mercy. I mean those who stand their sacred ground amid the violence and toxicity of patriarchy and keep the world spinning in love. I mean those who sing the world into being. I mean those who hum and dance and breathe and move to the rhythms of God's grace.

While I'm certain there's a better word than *woman* for the wise, warrior, mother, mystic women of this book (and of this world), I continue to use it because it is the word I was given, and it's the one I keep choosing. I refuse to let patriarchy take what Eve embodied so beautifully in the garden all those many moons, myths, and mysteries ago when she reached for the fruit to feed herself and her family.

Black, Brown, and Indigenous women have been leading the way of divine feminine love forever. They are the ones who've shown us how to center and celebrate women's stories—stories that lead people to liberation and love. They are the ones who've shown us how to divest from patriarchal, white supremacist systems of oppression; and,

---

[12] Quoted in *The New School News*, "Teaching to Transgress: bell hooks Returns to The New School," Oct. 7, 2014. https://blogs.newschool.edu/news/2014/10/bellhooksteachingtotransgress/

instead, they circle up around the fires of justice, under the light of the moon, and dance their way to freedom. They are the leaders of maternal mental health work, reproductive justice, and Palestinian liberation. They are the ones in whose steps I follow.

This book, just like my first book and just like all work to name and reclaim women and our stories, is for the women who came before us, for the women who stand beside us, for our children, for ourselves, for everyone. May the stories of women be told and heard and told and heard and told and heard, again and again, so that we know from whom we come and to whom we belong, which is always and forever Love.

Amen.

Prologue

Imagine a woman describing the following scene. She may be one of your ancestors. She may be the mother you always wanted but never had. She may be you. She may be me. Perhaps she is all of us who long for the sacred presence of women to be named and reclaimed from our scriptures and everywhere. Perhaps she is all of us who long to give our children a woman-led faith.

It's dark when I roll to my side, press my hands to the earth, and push myself up. I rub my eyes, open my mouth, and yawn. Reaching my arms to the sky, I stretch and breathe, taking a few moments before standing upright.

I move my bed mat, placing it in the corner. Then, I grab the basket of supplies and a pitcher of water, and then I set out for the hillside.

My feet know the way. Having trod this path many times before, they relax into the ground and carry me closer and closer to the light.

As I crest the hill, I see a spark from the flame we've been tending. Night and day, we keep watch. Vigilant. Present. Together. The only reality is our presence. The only place is here.

Later, when I spread my mat again for a night's sleep, I will wrap my arms around my daughter. I will draw her close to me, and I will whisper into her ear: *In the beginning were the women. And the women were with God. And the women were of God.*

She won't know what I mean exactly. She may even be asleep and not hear me at all. But I like to think that somehow the vibration of the words I speak will sink into her skin, seep into her bones, snake their way to the river of her blood, taking root, making space, creating refuge.

So that one day when she's feeling a bit unsure, unmoored, lonely, and afraid, the whisper will rise from within her, blossoming into what she knows to be true—*In the beginning were the women. And the women were with God. And the women were of God.*

She will then take two stones, striking them against each other in a rhythmic, repetitive beat until they spark into flame, into fire.

The women will come from near and far, from outside and within. They will gather, as they've always done, with bread, water, and oil. They will hum and sing, they will dance and pray. They will tell their stories. They will live.

And the longer they listen and the closer they get to the flame, my daughter—*our* daughters—will know that they are bound to a lineage of love.

The longer they listen, the closer they get to the flame, my daughter, *our* daughters will know: *In the beginning were the women. And the women were with God. And the women were of God.*

Amen.

Part One

Matriarchs are those who mother the world into being and who keep it spinning with their love; they are not only the ones traditionally named and upheld as matriarchs, but they are also the ones who were often abused and disenfranchised by those with power, means, and privilege but who remained present and persistent in their pursuit of love and justice anyway. To hear their stories, names, and lives is to hear, see, and know a broader, more loving and justice-seeking understanding of God and of "motherhood."

Chapter One

Eve

First Mother | Genesis 1:26–27 and 3:1–7

Eve (name): of Hebrew origin "Chavah," which means "to breathe, to live, to give life"

* * *

Then God said, "Let us make humans in our image, according to our likeness, and let them have dominion over the fish of the sea, and over the birds of the air, and over the cattle, and over all the wild animals of the earth and over every creeping thing that creeps upon the earth."

So God created humans in his image,
in the image of God he created them;
male and female he created them.

—Genesis 1:26–27

Now the serpent was more crafty than any other wild animal that the Lord God had made. He said to the woman, "Did God say, 'You shall not eat from any tree in the garden'?" The woman said to the serpent, "We may eat of the fruit of the trees in the garden, but God said, 'You shall not eat of the fruit of the tree that is in the middle of the garden, nor shall you touch it, or you shall die.'" But the serpent said to the woman, "You will not die, for God knows that when you eat of it your eyes will be opened, and you will be like God, knowing good and evil." So when the woman saw that the tree was good for food and that it was a delight to the eyes and that the tree was to be desired to make one wise, she took of its fruit and ate, and she also gave some to her husband, who was with her, and he ate. Then the eyes of both were opened, and they knew that they were naked, and they sewed fig leaves together and made loincloths for themselves.

—Genesis 3:1–7

* * *

EVE'S STORY

Imagine hearing Eve's story told by the women elders of your community. An oral herstory. An attempt to reimagine and reframe the first woman's beginnings and the first woman's legacy in which we follow.

Do you remember being born? Imagine your soft, wet, bloody flesh begging to be held. Your eyes, barely open. Your mouth, screaming to eat. Head down, face down, swimming toward the light. Not necessarily because you wanted to but because a force greater than you pushed you there.

Do you remember what it smelled like when you took your first breath? Probably metallic and mossy like wet grass on a forest floor. Sweet and fragrant like sugared lemon in the summertime.

Do you remember what it looked like when you first opened your eyes? Envision it being bright and blinding. Dark and dreary. Hazy and unclear.

Do you remember what you first heard? The sounds around you were your mama's wails. Your daddy's cries. Your midwife's coos. Your sister's shouts. Was a bird singing or a river running? Did anyone curse? Did anyone bless?

Do you remember what you first touched? Picture the dirt and dust. Skin and sweat. Flesh and fluid.

Do you remember what you first tasted? It most likely tasted like blood. Bile. Amniotic fluid. Sweet mother's milk. Your own salty tears.

It's likely that you don't consciously remember any of these details, but if you're lucky, someone has told you how you entered this world—who was there, how your mother pushed and breathed, what the room felt like, if there were tears or sighs or screams.

It's also likely that your body remembers your journey to earth, even if your mind doesn't. There's an intelligence to your flesh, a wisdom in your bone that speaks in a language all its own. If you can become quiet enough, you may be able to hear that language—a pulse, a beat, a rhythm, a song.

They say how we enter the world influences how we live, so to be born in a furious frenzy *may* mean we act furiously and frenzied when stressed. To be born in a quiet, undramatic, ordinary manner *may* mean we have a hard time getting motivated to do something difficult. I wonder: Does it matter how we were born? And if it does, what does Eve's birth say about her?

* * *

In the beginning there was darkness, and she was beautiful. Eve lived in the darkness of the earth, way down deep with the roots. In fact, Eve *was* one of the roots of God's tree. Its fruit, so luscious and abundant, Eve began to move toward it impulsively, without thought or plan. Twisting and turning through the dark earth, Eve reached the surface, pushing her way up and out.

With a grunt and a roar, she emerges, covered in mud and worm. She forms two legs, two feet, a torso and arms, a neck and a head, eyes, ears, mouth, teeth, fingers, breasts, armpits, and toes.

Standing upright, she is a person, though she does not yet know what that word means.

The fruit from the tree of God is scattered on the ground, hanging low from the branches, begging to be found.

Eve's stomach begins to rumble, and she suddenly feels a powerful urge to bring the fruit to her mouth. Eve is hungry. Eve is desiring. Eve is human.

She bites into the red, round yield, the juices dripping down her chin. Her sharp teeth pierce its waxy skin. Sweet and cold, its taste is a satisfying welcome to the place where dark and light meet, the trees' branches casting long shadows across the ground.

A smile creeps across her face. A breath, deep, long, and wide, spreads throughout her heart, lungs, and belly.

What do I call you? Eve asks the fruit.

Home, it replies.

* * *

Adam happens upon Eve in the late afternoon. The sun is low at the edge of the sky. Eve is eating.

"What is your name?" he asks, surprised yet comforted to see her.

"Eve," she replies. "Mother of all the living."

"I've been told we're not to eat this fruit," Adam says anxiously.

"Yes," says Eve. "I've heard that, too. But I say it breaks God's heart to pass by beauty and deliciousness without recognition and honor. I say eat and enjoy."[1]

"But you are not God," Adam says.

"No. But I do come from Her."

"But now that you know the tree's goodness, you will experience pain."

"Yes, dear Adam, now we will live fully."

Adam continues to ask questions, perplexed and uncertain, flummoxed and nervous.

"I do not understand," he says. "If we follow the rules, if we obey the commands, if we defer to another, then we will not suffer."

"Do you remember how you got here?" Eve asks.

"I do not."

"Close your eyes. Take a deep breath. Try."

Adam's eyes close. His breath, once shallow and short, begins to deepen and lengthen.

"I remember dirt. I remember bones. I remember the air," he says after a pregnant pause.

"What else do you remember?" Eve prods.

"I remember that when I first tried to walk, it hurt. Pain shot up my feet and legs, vibrating every muscle. I wobbled. I fell down again and again."

"Then what happened?"

---

[1] Inspired by *The Color Purple* by Alice Walker, in which she writes, "I think it makes God mad to pass by the color purple in a field and not notice it…" Alice Walker, *The Color Purple* (Orlando, FL: Harcourt Publishing, 1982), 196.

"I kept getting back up, and when I finally placed one foot in front of the other and took a few steps forward, it was as if I could see everything I'd ever wanted to see but didn't know I could."

"There you are," she says. "The pain *and* the bliss. The sorrow *and* the joy. Eating from this tree, enjoying this luscious fruit, saying yes to desire is not our sin but our salvation, not our evil but our goodness, not our punishment but our reward."

"Then how do you explain evil?" Adam asks.

"I don't," Eve replies.

"What do you mean?" he asks again.

"I mean it's not mine to understand. Is there evil? Yes. But do I need to understand it and place blame because of it? No. Because doing so will cause more pain. Instead, I accept what *is* and trust that God, in Her infinite wisdom, will see us through everything with love."

"That's too simple, too risky," he says.

"Maybe it is. But I'm willing to take the risk if it means experiencing joy and pleasure here and now."

Slowly, Adam reaches for a piece of fruit, brings it to his mouth, and takes a bite.

"This is really good," he says with a smile.

"I know," Eve says in return.

* * *

Labor begins with a slow, dull ache, and it grows into a continuous burn throughout Eve's entire body. Twisting and turning, she screams, "I'm on fire!" to no one and nothing.

Adam lays cool leaves upon her head. The trees offer shade. God gives breath.

Finally, with the help of God, Eve grunts and roars Cain into this world. Both mother and child are covered in mud and worm. It's like Eve is born from the dark ground yet again.

Adam uses a sharp rock to cut the cord, disconnecting Cain from Eve permanently. It happens so quickly, it takes Eve years to grieve the disconnection, the enduring separateness between her child and herself.

Adam worries endlessly about Eve's pain.

"Do you not remember that in the beginning I crawled and clawed my way out of the earth?" she asks him one night.

All Adam can do is look at Eve with eyes of wonder and fear.

Finally, Adam speaks the truth. "I will never know what it is to be as strong as you. My job, *our* job, is to bear witness and to bless. If we can't do that, we must do nothing at all."

* * *

In the end, Eve gave birth to three sons and three daughters. Cain, Abel, and Seth, her sons. Eden, Eva, and Eliana, her daughters.

Men feuded and fought. Women crafted and created on the sidelines of men's wars. Women had no need to seek pain outside of themselves. They knew pain intimately already, and it was their power, not their punishment. Unafraid to try new things, many learned to listen to their bodies, accept the gifts of Mother Earth, and eat and feed without rule or merit.

The Sacred Divine who gave birth to life first, even before Eve, was within creation from the very beginning. Walking. Grieving. Celebrating. Laboring. Dancing. Present and awake, the Sacred Divine sought not to destroy but to create, not to judge but to love.

* * *

To this very day, fruit trees grow across the lands, and in the fertile seasons their branches hang low with the product of their being. People reach up to pick the fruit or they bend low to gather the yield from the ground. While most of the time they place the harvest in baskets and barrels, every once in a while, a woman takes a bite from a juicy, cold, red piece. With the sap dripping down her chin, she honors the beginning, the ground from which Eve emerged.

From the very root of the Tree of God, Eve crawled her way up and out like the animal that she was. Desperate for the light, longing for food, she was the First Woman and the First Mother. Without her, the world, as we know it, would not have been born.

* * *

What if this were the story told about Eve, childbirth, and women? What if Eve's pain in childbirth (and in life) were not punishment for being curious, not condemnation for being hungry, but, instead, praise for being powerful, recognition for being true to herself? Might we dare to follow a God like that? Might we dare to follow women who follow God? And might our reimagination of Eve, might our retelling of good and evil, help to transform the world?

What story about Eve do you need to tell? What fruit do you long to eat? What love do you want to share? What power must you reclaim? Whatever it is, whatever sound it makes, and whatever meaning it produces, may it be liberating, not only for you, but for everyone.

LITURGY FOR MORNING PRAYER

OPENING

If you are gathered with others, position yourselves in a circle. Place a lit candle in the center. If you are alone, light a candle as a sign of connection to Mother God and the circle of women who join you, even here, even now, as you pray.

Morning Confession

In the beginning, You were there. **Mixing light and dark. Yielding fruit and freedom.**

Morning Prayer of Gratitude and Supplication

We thank you, God, for Eve, who, from the very beginning, has shown us how to live with perplexity and nuance, fire and inner strength.

Help us, God of Eve and fruit trees, mystery and love, to honor the lives from which we come, the lives for which we care, and the life which is ours to live, which is our own.

Like Eve, we now open ourselves fully to You. Give us strength. Give us wonder. Hold us in pain. Heal us in compassion. Walk alongside us this day and always. **Amen.**

Morning Psalm | Psalm 104: 1, 24–28, 31–35 (Inspired by the New Interpreter's Study Bible, New Revised Standard Version with the Apocrypha)

Bless our Creator! How abundant are Your works!

From Wisdom, we are born. The earth is full of Your goodness!

The elusive yet powerful sea that slips through our fingers yet bears enormous vessels is of You and in You.

You love everything, great and small.

From the earth, Eve emerged, showing all of us what it is to live.

Therefore, we will sing a new song as long as mountains quake; we will dance a new dance as long as trees sway.

We will invite saints and sinners alike to live the Way of Love.

We will bless. We will bear witness. We will believe in our goodness because You declared it so. Amen.

Scripture Reading: Genesis 1:26–31

The Word of Life. **Thanks be to God.**

A moment of quiet for prayer and reflection.

Prayers of the People

This morning's prayers of the people invite us to ask ourselves: Who is hungry? Whom do we need to feed? *In the quiet, consider these questions as prayers, and invite the Spirit to reveal to you whom you can feed from the abundance of God's bounty today.*

Song of Praise

Contemporary Connection

Take a few moments to watch and listen to "Armor" by Sara Bareilles and "Eve Was Black" by Allison Russell.[2] Imagine Eve singing these songs with her daughters, Eden, Eva, and Eliana. Allow these contemporary anthems to be part of your worshipful, prayerful, songful life.

The Prayer of the Women

Holy Mother of sand and sea,

to You all honor and praise.

When we cry out, You hear us.

When we ask for help, You help us.

When we long to be loved, You love us.

May mercy be offered to everyone.

May power and dominion over others cease.

May greed and violence end.

[2] Find links to each song at clairemckeeverburgett.com/music. There is also a QR code included in the Appendix at the end of this book that will take you to a public Spotify playlist of all the songs included in each liturgy. Enjoy!

May love live forever.
Birth us into a new world.
Help us make this one beautiful.
Stir us up. Settle us down.
Burn. Simmer. Refine.
When all else shakes, hold us steady.
When everyone else wants to blame,
remind us that in You there is only Love.
Our praise and our prayers are Yours, forever. Amen.

Closing Blessing

Go in peace to love, serve, and feed yourselves and the whole world. Amen.

REFLECTION QUESTIONS

1. What resonates with you about Eve's story? What feels redemptive? What feels challenging?
2. If you were to tell of Eve's beginning, what would you say? What is your story of Eve's birth?
3. When reading and praying along with Eve, Mother God, and the women, what sensations do you notice in your body?
4. What would it look like to rid yourself and others of blame?
5. What brings you unabashed joy? What keeps you from experiencing it fully?

PUBLIC WITNESS

Because what good are our prayers on Sunday if they make no meaning in our lives on Monday?

Part of our calling as people who claim to follow a God of love, justice, and mercy is to connect what we pray, sing, and hear on Sundays (or the day we set aside to worship God) to the whole of our lives. How does what we pray one day affect where we spend our time and financial resources on another day? How does praying for, about, and with women affect how we vote and whom we serve? God's loving call in Deuteronomy 6:5, "You shall love the Lord your God with all your heart, all your soul, and all your strength," commands us to integrate our faith into every aspect of our lives, which includes bearing witness to the good, necessary, and powerful work of justice-seeking, beauty-creating, love-making women in the world today.

Just as it is essential that we hear Eve's story in her words, so it's also essential that we empower girls and young women to tell their stories, use their voices, and share their creativity with the world. **Girls Write Nashville** is an organization doing just that as it empowers expression through songwriting, production, mentorship, and creative community for teen artists. Working within creative and expressive justice to be co-conspirators for youth mental health, **Girls Write Nashville** is a social impact organization allied with community schools to create safe and trauma-informed opportunities for youth.

Just as Eve seeks to feed herself and her family, **She Feeds the World** works to improve the food security and nutrition of poor, rural households, by emphasizing small-scale female producers.

Learn more about these organizations. Discover groups and faith communities in your area doing the work of justice, creativity, and feeding of the hungry. Connect. Learn. Give. Grow.[3]

---

[3] McKeever-Burgett, Claire, *Public Witness Woman-Led Nonprofits, https://www.clairemckeeverburgett.com/public-witness, accessed July 10, 2025.*

Chapter Two

Hagar

Forced Mother | Genesis 16; Genesis 21:1-21

Hagar (name): of Hebrew origin meaning "to flee" or "to be forsaken"

Content Warning: Sexual Violence

* * *

Hagar gave this name to the LORD who spoke to her, "You are the God who sees me," for she said, "I have now seen the One who sees me." That is why the well was called Beer Lahai Roi (well of the Living One who sees me); it is still there, between Kadesh and Bered.

—Genesis 16:13–14

God heard the boy crying, and the angel of God called to Hagar from heaven and said to her, "What is the matter, Hagar? Do not be afraid; God has heard the boy crying as he lies there. Lift the boy up and take him by the hand, for I will make him into a great nation."

Then God opened her eyes and she saw a well of water. So she went and filled the skin with water and gave the boy a drink.

God was with the boy as he grew up. He lived in the desert and became an archer. While he was living in the Desert of Paran, his mother got a wife for him from Egypt.

—Genesis 21:17–21

* * *

HAGAR'S STORY

Hagar's story is recorded in interview format, so that we receive Hagar's perspective on life as an enslaved woman, mother, and matriarch firsthand. Like the first-person slave narratives of the

Federal Writers' Project of 1936–1938, the hope is to hear Hagar's story clearly and, in so doing, understand her life anew.

What is your name, and what do you know about the meaning of your name?

My name is Hagar. I am the forsaken, fleeing, forced mother, which my name means. Master Abram and his wife, Sarai, renamed me when I was captured from Egypt, my home. Though I don't remember the name my mama gave me, I like to imagine it was Imara, meaning "brave one."

What was it like to be a slave in ancient Israel?

Just like people traded horses and mules, they traded people like me. Bought and sold and hired out, we were moved around based on what the masters required. I wasn't given any wage. They thought a tarp to sleep under and a mat to sleep on were enough.

Our kin were split up, scattered to the ends of the earth so nobody knew where anybody else was. My mama didn't know where my daddy or me ended up. I was eight years old the last time I saw them both. That's what it was like to be a slave: your people disappeared before your very eyes.

I wanted to learn how to speak Hebrew so I could better understand what the master and his people were saying, but I was always working. No time to learn a new language; no energy to listen or learn, even if the master had let me. They kept us busy and bone-tired, hoping our weariness would keep us from running away.

To be a woman and a slave meant work in the fields *and* work as a wife. The master took many of us as his own, because he and his people believed in a god that demanded male offspring. The more, the better.

At all costs. I wondered, *What kind of god was that?*

Being a wife to a master also meant serving as a handmaid to the master's original Hebrew wife, the woman of the household. Sarai, in my case. Far as I could tell, she didn't have much power if she couldn't give the master his sons, so she lived in desperation and fear, acting out her meanest ways on us *other* wives.

She forced us to have sex with her husband. Forced us to clean up her messes. Forced us to watch her eat what we couldn't. Forced us to feed children that weren't our own.

You think a mule would be a worker if it weren't forced to work? You think a horse would carry loads of goods if it weren't required to carry them? Nah. The mule would huddle with its pack under a shade tree. The horse would run wild across an open plain.

Don't believe people when they try to tell you what someone or something else likes. Unless you hear it from the horse's mouth, it probably isn't true.

'Cause Master Abram and his woman, Sarai, didn't see it as forcefulness. They convinced themselves we *wanted* to be mothers. They deluded themselves into thinking we *needed* to be rescued. They were certain they were our saviors, and we were the ones who needed saving.

What was it like when you learned you were pregnant with Ishmael?

When I showed up pregnant, the woman in charge acted like I wanted to have the master's baby.

If I said, "That's not true. You forced me to do it. He fooled himself into thinking this was God's will," I'd be set on fire.

"You aren't remembering correctly, Hagar. You've forgotten the truth, Hagar. The problem is you, Hagar."

She'd spit my name like it was too much saliva in her mouth, the hate dripping down her chin.

So, I kept quiet and said nothing at all.

* * *

"I need to get rid of my pregnancy," I whispered to another slave girl one night. I'd heard she'd helped other women in similar situations.

The next night, I found calendula and wormwood tucked under my pillow. My grandmother used to say these plants would make a pregnant woman bleed.

All they did for me was make me sick.

My belly grew. My rage simmered. My fear stewed.

So, what did you do? Where did you go?

I snuck out of camp one night when everyone else was asleep. I embodied the name they'd given me, and I fled. I found myself in the desert, alone. I had no plan; I only knew being away from my masters, dead, would be better than staying with them, alive.

It's been said you met God in the desert. A lot of lore surrounds you and your story. Tell us what happened, and tell us what made you go back?

The sun hung high in the sky, burning my dark skin even darker. Thirsty, tired, alone, I took a rest against a rock.

That's when I hear a voice.

"Child, where are you going? Why on earth are you here?"

That's when I say back, plain as day, " 'Cause I want to be free."

"Do you feel free?" the voice asks in a tone that reminds me of my mama's, indignant and curious at the same time.

"I don't know what I feel but tired," I speak. "You gonna save me?"

"I'm not gonna leave you, that's for sure."

"So I'm just gonna have the master's baby? I'm just gonna become a mama when I don't wanna be one?" I ask whoever, whatever will listen.

"Your baby is Ishmael, because God hears that baby and God hears you." The voice is soft and subtle, though I don't have any trouble hearing it. "Give birth to Ishmael. Your descendants will grow into a multitude; You will be their matriarch."

"Are you God?" I ask.

"Who do you think I am?" the voice asks me back.

"You're the one who sees me," I say after a long piece of quiet.

What was it like to be seen by God? What was it like to name God?

Everybody always acts like me naming God was some preconceived notion. But at that moment, it was the most natural thing I could do. Because God was more like Mama. Giving my baby a name. Reminding me I wasn't alone. Mama God saw me, and so I told her so.

As for Mama seeing me, well, I guess it was like when you finally learn how to write and spell your own name.

I-M-A-R-A.

H-A-G-A-R.

You write the letters. You see them on the page. You say them out loud. The way you see those letters that make a word that makes you is, well, magic.

How did I do it? You wonder. *What else can I write?* You ask. *What more do I have to say?* Your curiosity awakened, alive.

You returned to Abram and Sarai, pregnant with Ishmael, seen by God. What happened next?

In a dream I swim in the sea and walk in the desert at the same time. When I wake up, my bed mat is soaked with blood.

"Help!" I scream.

Into a ravine, the women take me, and I push Ishmael out of my body, onto the earth. He's round, red, and screaming. The child I never wanted is here.

The master's wife pushes Isaac out of her body, too. Not the same night that I give birth, but close to it because her baby is brought to me for feeding. Ishmael on one breast; Isaac on the other. They share a daddy but have different mamas. For a minute, I wonder if they'll be friends.

Doesn't take long for Ish and me to make the first wife mad. Did master like us more? Did she worry Isaac bonded with me because I nursed him? There she went again, feeding on fear and desperation.

This time, though, I'm not afraid.

One of those cool mornings before it gets blazing hot, master comes to me and says, "You have to leave."

He throws a knapsack on the ground. We have a small container of water, some bread, and a blanket.

"Go," he commands. "Go."

You have a baby still reliant on your body to survive, and you're cast out into the wilderness. What did you do? How did you survive?

Mama God is how we survived. It's not like She only sees you once and you're done. She sees you always, is with you always. Her love is present even when you want to die and even when you do.

I walk with Ish tied to my back for days. My feet bleed. My lungs wheeze. My thighs chafe. Ish screams. My breasts are as dry as the desert. I have nothing for him. The last drop of water absorbs into our dying flesh.

I leave him.

"I can't watch you die." I can hardly get it out.

He's screaming. I start running. I trip over a small rock and slide across the rough sand.

I will not get up. I will not move again. Here is where Ish and I will die, and I'm okay with that.

"Honey, what happened?" I hear the voice interrupt my sobs.

She knows I can't talk. She knows I want to die.

"Listen, here's what's gonna happen. I'm gonna help you up, and I'm gonna carry you back to Ishmael. None of us is gonna die today, you hear?"

Like a limp rag, I hang in Her arms as she lays me in a pool of cold water. Startled by the cold wet, I'm shocked back to reality.

Ish screams. *Fill the pouch with water. Give him a drink.* I think. Then, I do.

There I am in the middle of the desert with a kid I never wanted but who is mine, being carried by Mama God, watering my son and me back to life.

What's it like to grow old, to meet your grandchildren and great grandchildren? Is God true to God's promise?

Mama God is true, so yes, Her promise is true.

Ish becomes an archer. He marries. They have kids. The kids grow up and have more kids. And on and on it goes. To think it started with such terror and pain only to be transformed into something else entirely.

Growing old, my grandchildren and great-grandchildren run

circles around me while I sit still. I watch. I listen. I absorb. Every once in a while, one of them asks me a question, and I speak.

"Ooo, honey," I say to my great-granddaughter, Imara, slapping my knee to signal she just asked me a doozey. "You really wanna know where you come from?" She nods.

"You come from a great-grandmother who never wanted to be one," I tell the truth. "You come from a great-grandmother who named God in the desert 'cause She saw me. You come from a woman who named God and lived."

"How did *that* happen?" she asks as her eyes widen, her breath quickening.

"There's no real telling," I say with a sigh. "There's just livin' and trustin' that Mama God will show up, and, for me, She always did. For me, She always does."

"What about for me?" Imara asks. "Will God show up for me?"

"Of course she will," I sigh.

"How do you know?" she asks, pressing me for proof.

"It's like how you know how to spell your own name," I say. "I-M-A-R-A. As good as you know how to do that, as good as you know how to say it, that's how certain Mama God has been, is, and forever will be with you."

Imara nods and then joins the other kids playing in the dirt.

Later that night, as I tend the fire, I can hear Imara from her tent as she spells out her name, again and again. I-M-A-R-A. *IMARA*. Repeatedly she spells the letters and then says her name.

It's her prayer. And it becomes mine, too, as I stare into the flame, knowing what it is to be seen and known by Mama God, praying that Imara will know the same.

LITURGY FOR MIDDAY PRAYER

OPENING

If you are gathered with others, position yourselves in a circle. Place a lit candle in the center. If you are alone, light a candle as a sign of connection to Mother God and the circle of women who join you, even here, even now, as you pray.

Call to Prayer

Mama God, help us to look you in the eyes in this midday moment of prayer.

Help us to see You, and in seeing You, help us to see ourselves and others more clearly.

Amen.

Prayer at Midday

El Roi, the God who Sees,

This midday moment of prayer reminds us of Hagar in the desert.

It reminds us that many, like Hagar, are lost and afraid, and in need of Your help.

You call us to pause from our work and our lives and be renewed to love others and to see others as You see them.

You call us to pause from our work and our lives so that we, like Hagar, might see You.

May it be so forever. Amen.

Psalm 27:7–14 (inspired by the Common English Bible translation)

Hear us when we speak, O God.

Have mercy on us and answer us.

Our hearts long to seek Your face,

And so Your face we will seek.

Like Hagar in the desert, we boldly say,

"Do not hide your face from us any longer;

Do not turn away from us in anger;

Help us! Save us! Mama God, be our Savior!"

Though Hagar was abused, raped, and abandoned,

Though she was forgotten, mistreated, and forsaken,

You held her, loved her, and received her with mercy.

You do the same for us.
Teach us your Way of Love.
Show us water in the deserts of our lives.
Save us from all systems
  that seek to kill and destroy anyone or anything.
Make us confident of Your goodness, Mama God.
Lead us to the land of the living.
We will wait for Mama God.
Hagar waited and was seen.
Hagar's heart was strong, her will was true.
Mama God delivered her. Mama God delivers us.
Alleluia. Amen.
Pause here for a moment of quiet.

Scripture Reading: Genesis 16:13–14; Genesis 21:17–21

A living, breathing word.
Thanks be to God.

Song of Praise

In the Beginning

Claire K. McKeever-Burgett

Contemporary Connection

Take a few moments to watch and listen to "To Zion" by Lauryn Hill and "PROTECTOR" by Beyonce.[4] Imagine Hagar singing these songs to Ishmael as she hid in the hot desert. Invite the vibrations of the music and the melodies to join your prayerful, worshipful, songful life.

The Prayer of the Women

Holy Mother of sand and sea,
to You all honor and praise.
When we cry out, You hear us.
When we ask for help, You help us.
When we long to be loved, You love us.
May mercy be offered to everyone.
May power and dominion over others cease.
May greed and violence end.
May love live forever.
Birth us into a new world.
Help us make this one beautiful.
Stir us up. Settle us down.
Burn. Simmer. Refine.
When all else shakes, hold us steady.
When everyone else wants to blame,
remind us that in You there is only Love.
Our praise and our prayers are Yours, forever. Amen.

REFLECTION QUESTIONS

1. What resonates with you about Hagar's story? What feels redemptive? What feels challenging?
2. When reading and praying along with Hagar, Mama God, and the women, what sensations do you notice in your body?

---

[4] McKeever-Burgett, Claire, *Music for Contemporary Connections,* https://www.clairemckeeverburgett.com/*music, accessed July 10, 2025.*

3. What would you name God if you could?
4. What would you say to God if you met God face to face?
5. From what has God saved you? From what have you saved yourself?

PUBLIC WITNESS

Because what good are our prayers on Sunday if they make no meaning in our lives on Monday?

Part of our calling as people who claim to follow a God of love, justice, and mercy is to connect what we pray, sing, and hear on Sundays (or the day we set aside to worship God) to the whole of our lives. How does what we pray one day affect where we spend our time and financial resources on another day? How does praying for, about, and with women affect how we vote and who we serve? God's loving call in Deuteronomy 6:5, "You shall love the Lord your God with all your heart, all your soul, and all your strength," commands us to integrate our faith into every aspect of our lives, which includes bearing witness to the good, necessary, and powerful work of justice-seeking, beauty-creating, love-making women in the world today.

Planned Parenthood and **Sister Song** are two woman-centered and woman-led organizations, which promote the work of reproductive justice and a woman's right to choose what is best for her body, two issues that Hagar faced in her life centuries ago and that women still face today. **Planned Parenthood Federation of America, Inc. (PPFA)** protects and expands access to sexual and reproductive health care and education and provides support to its member affiliates. **Planned Parenthood affiliates** are separately incorporated public charities that operate health centers across the US as trusted sources of health care and education for people of all genders.

Sister Song is a national membership organization based in the South that is building an effective network of individuals and organizations to improve institutional policies and systems that affect the reproductive lives of marginalized communities.

Learn more about these organizations and how you can get involved with Planned Parenthood and other groups doing the work of reproductive justice in your area. Connect. Learn. Give. Grow.[5]

---

[5] McKeever-Burgett, Claire, *Public Witness Woman-Led Nonprofits,* https://www.clairemckeeverburgett.com/public-witness, *accessed July 10, 2025.*

Chapter Three

Aholibamah | Judith | Astarte

Scandalized Mother | Genesis 26:34–35 and 36:1–8

Aholibamah (name): of Hebrew origin meaning "tent of the high place" or "my tabernacle is exalted"

Judith (name): of Hebrew origin meaning "to be praised"

Astarte (name): Canaanite goddess of love, fertility, and war

* * *

When Esau was forty years old, he married Judith daughter of Beeri the Hittite, and also Basemath daughter of Elon the Hittite. They were a source of grief to Isaac and Rebekah.

—Genesis 26:34–35

These are the descendants of Esau (that is, Edom). Esau took his wives from the Canaanites: Adah daughter of Elon the Hittite, Aholibamah daughter of Anah son of Zibeon the Hivite, and Basemath, Ishmael's daughter, sister of Nebaioth. Adah bore Eliphaz to Esau; Basemath bore Reuel; and Aholibamah bore Jeush, Jalam, and Korah. These are the sons of Esau who were born to him in the land of Canaan.

Then Esau took his wives, his sons, his daughters, and all the members of his household, his cattle, all his livestock, and all the property he had acquired in the land of Canaan; and he moved to a land some distance from his brother Jacob. For their possessions were too great for them to live together; the land where they were living could not support them because of their livestock. So Esau settled in the hill country of Seir; Esau is Edom.

—Genesis 36:1–8

* * *

ASTARTE'S STORY

I was both a hunter and a gatherer. A woman had to be both to keep the generations alive. Who else was going to feed the hungry mouths? Who else was going to ensure the lineages continued but a woman, a mother, a matriarch?

Not much has been said about me other than that Isaac and Rebecca didn't want Esau to marry me and that I was unfaithful to Esau throughout our marriage. After all, in one biblical passage I'm named Judith, suggesting that Esau changed my name to a Hebrew one to appease his parents. In another passage, I'm named Aholibamah, suggesting I built temples to other gods.[6]

In each story, men named me according to *their* needs and interpretation.

What would my name be if I had the power to name myself?

I am Astarte, named after the Canaanite goddess of hunting and love. Killing the animals that fed my family always felt like an act of love. What else would it be?

As the bleeding, dead animal lay before me, I would kneel in front of it, as my grandmother and mother taught me. Like kneeling at an altar. Like kneeling in birth. Like I was ready to both weep and pray all at once.

Placing my hands in its pooling blood, I would pray with the animal and the spirits, "Thank you. Bless you. May you be at peace."

For the animal had a soul, too. And though it was part of the natural order for us to kill animals to eat and survive, honoring their sacrifice was an essential part of the cycle of both life and death. It was the way of my ancestors, and I followed their lead.

My wily, agile body, thick with strong muscles, guided me home. Jumping over rocks, dodging holes some animal dug in the ground, I knew the land like I knew my mother's hand.

---

[6] Kadari, Tamar, "Esau, Wives of: Midrash and Aggadah," in *The Shalvi/Hyman Encyclopedia of Jewish Women*, Jewish Women's Archive, 2009, accessed July 15, 2025, https://jwa.org/encyclopedia/article/esau-wives-of-midrash-and-aggadah.

Arriving back at camp with the animal's dead body slung across my shoulders, I'd locate the butcher tent. There, I would find the tools needed to prepare the meat for cooking or preserving.

My life was about so much more than having sex with Esau to give him male sons whose names are recorded in the scriptures. My daughters? Their names are only found within my heart. My life with its beauty and complexity, sorrow and joy? My story will be told now.

* * *

Winding through the thick brush, chasing after a lamb gone rogue, I trip over a stone. My face hits the earth with a thud. Immediately I taste blood. With a groan, I start to push myself up when I hear a crackling behind me.

Quickly, I jump to my feet. Turning, my spear lifted and ready, I see a large, hairy, red man.

"I come in peace," the red man says. "Are you a hunter?" he asks.

I give a slight nod, not wanting to speak.

"I don't know many women who hunt," he says with a chuckle.

"How unfortunate for you," I say without thinking.

He raises his eyebrows and grins. "May I hunt with you?" he asks.

"Fine," I say. "But you'll lead, and I'll bring up the rear."

"Keeping your eyes on me, eh?" he retorts with a cock of his head.

Rolling my eyes, I thrust my spear toward him. "Go," I command.

* * *

This is how we begin, Esau and me. Hunting together. He is amazed at how adept I am, how quiet, how free. I am annoyed to have a partner, though together we *do* bring home more food for our families, which helps immensely.

Esau doesn't know anything about my personal life, and I don't know anything about his. We keep quiet while hunting, allowing the silence to guide us toward our prey. So, to say I am shocked the day I return to camp to hear from my father that I will marry Esau is an understatement.

"What do you mean?" I stammer.

"I've made an agreement with Esau. It's best for all of us if you just go."

"What about my girls?" I cry. "Who will care for them?"

"We will be safe when you marry Esau. This is how we will keep the peace, fragile as it is. Your daughters will stay with your mother and me. They'll be okay. So will you."

I stumble back to my tent, too angry to cry. Buckling over in pain, I feel like someone punched me in the gut. Breath escapes me. My heart, if it were a clay pot, would be shattered into a thousand pieces on the ground. My daughters hold my entire heart.

* * *

In the end, I married Esau because I had to, for the safety of my family. I said goodbye to my daughters, Azizos, Ashima, and Ishat, named after the Canaanite goddesses of the morning star (because Azizos was born as the sun was rising in the east), the Canaanite goddess of fate (because Ashima was born with a third eye that could see things clearly), and the Canaanite goddess of fire (because Ishat was born by the fire on a bitterly cold night). I told them I would always be with them, even if not physically present. I wept as I walked away.

* * *

Here's how the rumors about me began.

I didn't follow the rules. I hunted instead of gathered. I didn't bow to male gods. I listened to my body's ancient wisdom, and I let it lead. I uttered my daughters' names like the prayers that they were, and I treated them just as sacredly as I treated my sons. I named myself, and I insisted people call me by that name and no other.

Esau's parents, Isaac and Rebecca, knew I wasn't a rule follower, which is why they despised Esau for marrying me. Sure, they hated that I was Canaanite, but they also hated that I was strong and held my head high, that when Esau called me Judith, I said, "My name is Astarte." When Esau said I was "Aholibamah," I insisted, "My name is Astarte."

Rebecca would whisper in Esau's ear, "She's sleeping with other men. You cannot trust her."

Isaac would tell Esau to follow me, to keep tabs on where I went, what I was doing, and who I was spending time with.

What Esau discovered didn't surprise him.

He found me, alone in the woods, close to nature, listening to the wisdom of my ancestors. He found me sneaking back to my family's camp to catch a glimpse of my daughters who now had children of their own. He found me praying to a God I could believe in. She had wide hips, a soft belly, and open arms. Her face, dark, her eyes bright. She welcomed me as I was.

* * *

It is late one night, and the moon is full of light. Both Esau and I lie awake next to one another. Though there are only inches between us, it might as well be a wide chasm without a bridge given how far we are from each other.

"I know where you go," he says to the room.

"I know you know," I say in return.

It is quiet for a long time. Only the rhythm of our breath, in and out, in and out, fills the room.

"You don't care that I know?" he asks, desperate for me to need his affirmation and approval.

"I stopped caring a long time ago, Esau. I am who I am. Always have been."

Esau rolls away from me, and that is the last we ever speak about it. A silent alliance, a quiet truce. He knows he can't change me, and I know my fate is sealed with him as his wife, that the only sliver of freedom I have is in wandering in the woods, worshipping a trustworthy God, and catching holy glimpses of my daughters.

This is the small gift Esau gives me in return for giving him three sons—Jeush, Jaalam, and Korah. Sealed as a matriarch in the biblical line, I fulfill my duty and try to keep the world, as I know it, spinning in love.

* * *

Wandering through the brush, I reach for my spear. Lifting my arm, I hurtle the spear through the air. It soars toward the animal, and for a moment, all is quiet, save the subtle whistle from its piercing of the air. I hear the animal squeal. I smell its blood.

Though I am old, I can still move swiftly toward the animal, finishing the job of its killing.

As I yank the spear from its dead body, I hear a crackling in the brush behind me. Without turning around, I know Esau stands behind me.

With a slight turn of my head, I say, "Want to hunt with me?"

Without hesitation he says, "I thought you'd never ask."

* * *

Rebecca and Isaac never accepted me. They continued to despise me in their family line till the day they died. Thankfully, Esau and I had the hunt to keep us close. Perhaps that's how, in the end, my name remained in the litany of matriarchs. Aholibamah is what the records say even though Astarte is my name, and Azios, Ashima, and Ishat are my daughters' names.

Though my heart was shattered when I was ripped from them to marry Esau, I pray we are known in the story and heard in the songs, not so much for our sake, but for the sake of scandalized women everywhere, for the sake of women who are questioned and followed, for the sake of women who don't obey the rules, for the sake of women who hunt and kill, for the sake of women who provide and love. I pray that in naming me in the prayers and liturgies of the faith, even by a name that I did not choose for myself, the age-old story will expand and the lineage of the people of God might include many more than we've ever known.

I pray. I hunt. I hope. Amen.

LITURGY FOR MIDDAY PRAYER

OPENING

If you are gathered with others, position yourselves in a circle. Place a lit candle in the center. If you are alone, light a candle as a sign of connection to Mother God and the circle of women who join you, even here, even now, as you pray.

Call to Prayer

In God, we find a safe place to dwell–
to hear our stories anew, to upend old narratives,
to learn new names, to pause, to listen, to breathe.
Alleluia. Amen.

Prayer at Midday

God of many places, names, stories, and loves–
As we pause at midday to hear Astarte's story
and to expand our hearts and minds to new ideas,
be with us and in us, we pray.
All that has been,
all that is,
all that will be
is Yours.
Therefore, we can trust that
all shall be well and all manner of
thing shall be well.[7]
Amen.

[7] Quoted by Julian of Norwich, a fourteenth-century English mystic and theologian. Julian, Anchoress at Norwich, *Revelations of Divine Love*, ed. Grace Warrack (Methuen & Company, 1901), 56, Project Gutenberg, accessed July 15, 2015, https://www.gutenberg.org/files/52958/52958-h/52958-h.htm

Psalm 55:16–19 (inspired by the *Common English Bible* translation)

In the woods, in the valley,
When we sleep, when we rise,
At midday or midnight,
Anytime, anywhere, we can call out to God
and She will save us by showing us
all the ways we are loved.
In desperation and in fear,
When our names are erased and
Our stories unheard,
At our waking, at our sleeping,
Anytime, anywhere, we can call out to God
And She will save us by showing us
All the ways we are loved.
In joy and in sorrow,
When we hunt and when we gather,
At birth and at death,
Anytime, anywhere, we can call out to God
And She will save us by showing us
All the ways we are loved.

Scripture Reading: Genesis 26:34–35 and 26:1–8

A living, breathing Word.

Thanks be to God.

Hold a few moments of quiet for prayer and reflection.

Song of Praise

In the Beginning

Claire K. McKeever-Burgett

Contemporary Connection

*Take a few minutes to watch and listen to "***Flawless" by Beyoncé, ft. Chimamanda Ngozi Adichie and "The Daughters" by Little Big Town.*[8] *Consider the ways in which both Beyoncé and Chimamanda subvert the age-old narrative of what women are supposed to do and be in many of the same ways as Aholibamah/Judith/Astarte. Hear the words of "The Daughters" and meditate on Astarte's daughters who were never named in the stories of old. Imagine Astarte singing these songs to and with her daughters. Invite these songs to be part of your prayerful, worship, songful life.*

The Prayer of the Women

Holy Mother of sand and sea,
to You all honor and praise.
When we cry out, You hear us.
When we ask for help, You help us.
When we long to be loved, You love us.

[8] McKeever-Burgett, Claire, *Music for Contemporary Connections*, https://www.clairemckeeverburgett.com/*music, accessed July 10, 2025.*

May mercy be offered to everyone.
May power and dominion over others cease.
May greed and violence end.
May love live forever.
Birth us into a new world.
Help us make this one beautiful.
Stir us up. Settle us down.
Burn. Simmer. Refine.
When all else shakes, hold us steady.
When everyone else wants to blame,
remind us that in You there is only Love.
Our praise and our prayers are Yours, forever. Amen.

REFLECTION QUESTIONS

The following questions are meant to deepen and expand, invite and beckon thoughtful, compassionate, and curious responses to the story and liturgy of Aholibamah/Judith/Astarte. Whether considering these questions on your own or in a group setting, create space for journaling, collaging, or painting in response to them. If engaging in group discussion, choose one or two questions, at most, to hold at the center of your sacred circle.

1. What resonates with you about Astarte's story? What feels redemptive? What feels challenging?
2. When reading and praying along with Astarte, Mother God, and the women, what sensations do you notice in your body?
3. What would your name be if you could name yourself today? If you would keep your name the same, why? If you would change it, why?
4. How might women's names and stories change if we'd always held the power to name ourselves and tell our own stories?
5. What might God be calling you to reconsider considering Astarte's name and story?

PUBLIC WITNESS

Because what good are our prayers on Sunday if they make no meaning in our lives on Monday?

Part of our calling as people who claim to follow a God of love, justice, and mercy is to connect what we pray, sing, and hear on Sundays (or the day we set aside to worship God) to the whole of our lives. How does what we pray one day affect where we spend our time and financial resources on another day? How does praying for, about, and with women affect how we vote and whom we serve? God's loving call in Deuteronomy 6:5, "You shall love the Lord your God with all your heart, all your soul, and all your strength," commands us to integrate our faith into every aspect of our lives, which includes bearing witness to the good, necessary, and powerful work of justice-seeking, beauty-creating, love-making women in the world today.

When I think of Astarte's story as a woman from a different land who had her name recorded for the purpose of highlighting the male lineage of the Hebrew people, I can't help but think of other conquered lands and the women living within them.

The United Nations Women's Peace and Humanitarian Fund supports local women's organizations in Palestine to prevent conflict, strengthen women's economic resilience, and to support active participation in peacebuilding. As of October 2023, the fund is also responding to the escalating crisis and humanitarian needs of women and children in Palestine.

Learn more about this humanitarian fund and the ongoing crisis for women and children in Palestine. Continue to seek out organizations in your own communities that engage in the work of advocacy and empowerment of all women, regardless of nationality or religion. Connect. Learn. Give. Grow.[9]

---

[9] McKeever-Burgett, Claire, *Public Witness Woman-Led Nonprofits, https://www.clairemckeeverburgett.com/public-witness, accessed July 10, 2025.*

Chapter Four

Bilhah and Zilpah

Forgotten Mothers | Genesis 30:1–13 and 1 Chronicles 7:13

Bilhah (name): of Hebrew origin meaning "troubled" or "timid"

Zilpah (name): of Hebrew origin meaning "to be given" or "to fall"

* * *

When Rachel saw that she bore Jacob no children, she envied her sister, and she said to Jacob, "Give me children, or I shall die!" Jacob became very angry with Rachel and said, "Am I in the place of God, who has withheld from you the fruit of the womb?" Then she said, "Here is my maid Bilhah; go in to her, that she may bear upon my knees and that I too may have children through her." So she gave him her maid Bilhah as a wife, and Jacob went in to her. And Bilhah conceived and bore Jacob a son. Then Rachel said, "God has judged me and has also heard my voice and given me a son"; therefore she named him Dan. Rachel's maid Bilhah conceived again and bore Jacob a second son. Then Rachel said, "With mighty wrestlings I have wrestled with my sister and have prevailed," so she named him Naphtali.

When Leah saw that she had ceased bearing children, she took her maid Zilpah and gave her to Jacob as a wife. Then Leah's maid Zilpah bore Jacob a son. And Leah said, "Good fortune!" So she named him Gad. Leah's maid Zilpah bore Jacob a second son. And Leah said, "Happy am I! For the women will call me happy," so she named him Asher.

—Genesis 30:1–13

The sons of Naphtali: Jahziel, Guni, Jezer, and Shallum, the descendants of Bilhah.

—1 Chronicles 7:13

* * *

BILHAH and ZILPAH'S STORY

We are seven and five when we learn that Laban is our father. He loved our mother, who was also a slave and who had recently died of a fever.

He's telling us this as we sit on the floor of our tent wondering where our mama is. He's trying to be gentle, though his long beard and creased skin screams of someone who's lived on the land most of their lives, hardened by the elements. He's speaking quickly. He wants it to be done.

"If Mama isn't here, where is she?" we ask together. Mama was always saying Zilpah and I shared one mind and one heart.

"With God," Laban says.

"Where is God?" we ask in unison again.

"Above us," he says.

"In the clouds?" we wonder aloud.

"Sure."

Abruptly, he stands. We cut our dark eyes at one another, unsure whether to call him master or daddy or something else entirely. Neither of us wants to ask.

"The other women will see to it that you're fed," he says, turning to go.

Zilpah and I begin to cry, our noses dripping snot. One of us sniffles. Laban turns toward us.

"You can be sad as long as it doesn't affect your work." The tent opening flaps in the breeze as he leaves.

I suppose, in his way, that was Laban showing us love. Lesser men wouldn't have visited us at all.

* * *

Zilpah is the first to bleed at the age of eleven. We try to hide it for fear that they'll separate us from each other. It works for a few months, but then they discover her bloody rags and move her to another tent. They allot her to Leah, who, it turns out, is our sister.

The less and less we see of one another, the more our hearts and minds become one. I lie in bed at night imagining each of our hearts growing large, reaching across fields and tents and brush to connect. We grow a super heart. It beats for both of us. I can feel Zilpah with me every time I take a wet cloth to one of the women's faces, preparing the woman for bed. Zilpah can feel me every time she helps Leah get dressed. Each of us wonders, *Does the other know I think of her?* The answer is yes.

I eventually begin bleeding, too, and am allotted to Rachel. She and Leah are now the wives of Jacob, the patriarch. They don't seem to care that we share a father. In fact, they pretend that we're orphans and have no father or mother at all.

We didn't just fall from the sky, I think, but never say.

* * *

The night is young when I am awakened by another handmaid. She shakes me furiously.

"Bilhah, Bilhah, wake up! Rachel needs you!"

Groggy, I wrap myself in a shawl, cover my head, and walk to Rachel's tent. Bowing as I enter, I ask, "What do you need?"

I lift my head ever so slightly to see her face. Her eyes dart every which way, unable to find a resting place. She is nervous and angry. A slight twitch just above the right side of her face makes me wonder, *Who died?*

"Jacob will come to your tent tonight, and he will have sex with you." Her voice cracks at the end of the statement.

She continues, though her voice shakes.

"God willing, you will become pregnant, and when it's time for you to give birth, you will do so upon my knees. The child will not be your own. The child will be mine."

With a slight nod of my head, averting my eyes from hers, I turn to go.

"Do you understand?" she spits at my back. "Tell me you understand," she commands.

Without turning around, I whisper, "I understand."

* * *

I'm young and fertile and become pregnant in no time. As the baby grows inside of me, my back aches and my hips cry. In the final month before I give birth, I feel as if my entire inside might fall out of me.

When labor begins and it's obvious that I am progressing, I'm ushered into Rachel's room. She kneels in front of me. I squat and groan and breathe and, finally, push the baby onto her lap. For a moment, I see a wet and screaming baby boy, before Rachel takes him in her arms and says, "His name is Dan."

I'm given three days to heal from giving birth before they force me back into the fields. Someone must do the work.

* * *

I learn later that the same happened to Zilpah. Leah, though she already had male children, grew jealous of Rachel's bounty, and forced Zilpah to be with Jacob. Zilpah gave birth to Gad, her precious child whom Leah claimed as her own.

Our sons cannot survive without eating from our bodies. So, countless times a day we are called to feed our children. For a few blessed, holy moments, we are near our sons, skin to skin, face to face—a tiny respite from what feels like eternal separation.

I bear a second son for Jacob and Rachel, another child I do not get to name. Naphtali. Zilpah bears Jacob and Leah another one, as well. Asher. And though we grow them and feed them, they do not know us as their mothers, only as their caretakers.

We are mothers by proxy; we are mothers easily forgotten.

* * *

Time is a gift and a curse. Sometimes all you want is more time. Other times, all you want is time to evaporate. For Zilpah and me, time both evaporated and stretched on and on like a long road leading to nowhere.

Eventually, our sons returned to us. Leah and Rachel's sons gained their full energy and attention, so our sons needed our care, focus, and love. Eventually, I was named in the Chronicles as a matriarch, though most liturgies still ignore my existence. Zilpah does not receive a place in the story at all.

* * *

There is a moment later in our lives when Zilpah and I meet in an open field outside the main encampment. Locking eyes, we smile, take each other's hands, and begin walking toward the Eastern sun. Instinctively, we both stop at the same time, the summit of the hill round and wide. We open our arms, look up, and begin to laugh.

We laugh for hours. The oxygen leaves our lungs and returns to them repeatedly. The tears roll out the sides of our eyes. The muscles in our guts are sore from the visceral movement of joy. We are five and seven again, playing in the yard, joyful and unbound. Our mama is still alive.

Living a long time as enslaved women is a miracle. We're old. We're alive. We have something to laugh about; though, we're not entirely sure what. We're together. Not unheard of, but certainly rare.

Standing before the sun, I turn to Zilpah and say, "I will always remember."

She looks back at me, and says, "Me too."

We squeeze each other's hands. We promise each other, "We will meet every year in the same place and walk toward the same fiery sun as an act of remembrance, not only for ourselves, but for forgotten mothers everywhere."

It's our ritual of healing, resistance, and love until we die. And even then, we trust that the ritual continues as other women, forgotten by the world yet found by one another, follow in our footsteps.

LITURGY FOR EVENING PRAYER

OPENING

Set a table with bread and water. Light a candle. Breathe. Enter this sacred time with quietness and ease, trusting God among you and within you as you pray, as you eat, as you drink with God and the women.

Opening Proclamation

May the bread on this table remind us of the forgotten mothers throughout time.

May the water on this table remind us that we always can be forgiven for our complicity in systems that seek to control and dominate women.

May the light remind us of the women who carried the flame of love even when we ignored them or actively tried to hold them back.

May being together in the presence of God and one another be a place to start, and may we continue the work of reconciliation and love for all bodies, all people, everywhere. Amen.

Evening Prayer

We come to this time and place from hurried, harried days, begging for a moment in which we can settle ourselves and our hearts in the presence of God and the women, without whom we'd have very little, if anything, at all.

Every accolade, every error,

Every attagirl, every critique,

Every smile, every frown,

Every overflow, every emptiness,

we give to You, O God, Our Mother.

Wrapped in Your embrace.

Held in Your care.

Known in Your presence.

This day, this time, just as all days and all time,

are yours. **Amen.**

Psalm 147:1–6 (inspired by the Common English Bible translation)

As forgotten mothers and discarded women, we sing praises to Mother God because She has always been with us, our Comfort and our Guide.

She healed us after we were used and abused.

She restored us, though we were once exiled from our children.

Though our hearts were broken in two,

God bandaged them, soothing our wounds.

When we rested on the hillside, meditating on the stars,

God gave each one a name,

reminding us that just as the stars were not forgotten,

neither were we.

God, Our Mother, is fierce and strong.

Her ability to see into the heart of all things

is powerful, and it saves.

She helps the poor, the outcast, the enslaved.

She is for love and not wickedness.

She is for healing and not hurt.

Scripture Reading: Genesis 30:1–13 and 1 Chronicles 7:13

A living, breathing Word. **Thanks be to God.**

A moment of quiet for prayer and reflection.

Prayers with the Women

Before praying with the women, break some bread and eat it. Pour the cup and drink it. Trust these simple actions as embodied prayers of healing and love.

Someone, somewhere cannot see a way forward.

Mercy, Mother. Mercy.

Someone, somewhere fears what may happen on the other side.

Mercy, Mother. Mercy.

Someone, somewhere hides her children out of fear.

Mercy, Mother. Mercy.

Someone, somewhere boards a boat, chasing freedom.

Mercy, Mother. Mercy.

Someone, somewhere buries a child.

Mercy, Mother. Mercy.

Someone, somewhere cannot find their child, no matter how hard they try.

Mercy, Mother. Mercy.

Someone, somewhere weeps for what is lost.

Mercy, Mother. Mercy.

Someone, somewhere hardens and turns away from love.

Mercy, Mother. Mercy.

Someone, somewhere is hungry.

Mercy, Mother. Mercy.

Someone, somewhere feeds.

Mercy, Mother. Mercy.

Someone, somewhere is forgotten.

Mercy, Mother. Mercy.

Someone, somewhere is remembered.

Mercy, Mother. Mercy.

For all the someones who are somewhere,

with all the someones who are somewhere,

we pray, knowing we, too, are someone, somewhere

in need of prayer, safety, remembrance, food, freedom, and love.

Mercy, Mother. Mercy.

Amen.

Song of Praise

In the Beginning

Claire K. McKeever-Burgett

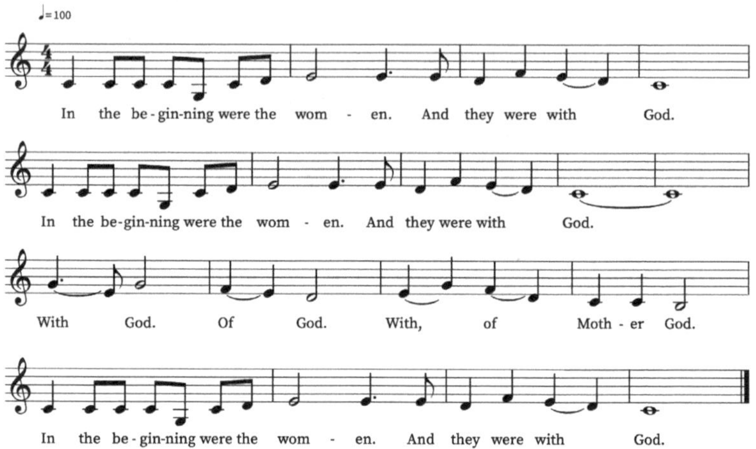

Contemporary Connection

Take a few moments to listen to and watch "Quiet" by MILCK and "Don't Forget Me" by Maggie Rogers.[10] *As you listen and watch, imagine Bilhah and Zilpah singing these songs together on the hillside as a reclamation of their agency and power in the face of cruelty and control. Invite these songs to be part of your prayerful, worshipful, songful life.*

The Prayer of the Women

Holy Mother of sand and sea,

to You all honor and praise.

When we cry out, You hear us.

When we ask for help, You help us.

When we long to be loved, You love us.

May mercy be offered to everyone.

May power and dominion over others cease.

May greed and violence end.

---

[10] McKeever-Burgett, Claire, *Music for Contemporary Connections*, https://www.clairemckeeverburgett.com/*music, accessed July 10, 2025.*

May love live forever.
Birth us into a new world.
Help us make this one beautiful.
Stir us up. Settle us down.
Burn. Simmer. Refine.
When all else shakes, hold us steady.
When everyone else wants to blame,
remind us that in You there is only Love.
Our praise and our prayers are Yours, forever. Amen.

Closing Blessing

Go forth, beloved, and be love to someone, somewhere,
even and especially if that someone, somewhere is you.
Amen.

REFLECTION QUESTIONS

The following questions are meant to deepen and expand, invite and beckon thoughtful, compassionate, and curious responses to the story and liturgy of Bilhah and Zilpah. Whether considering these questions on your own or in a group setting, create space for journaling, collaging, or painting in response. If engaging in group discussion, choose one or two questions, at most, to hold at the center of your sacred circle.

1. What resonates with you about Bilhah and Zilpah's story? What feels redemptive? What feels challenging?
2. When reading and praying with Bilhah and Zilpah, Mother God, and the women, what sensations do you notice in your body?
3. Recall a time when you were forgotten or left out of a story, an event, or a relationship. What did you feel? What did it make you want to do? Where was God in the midst?
4. What might God be inviting you to learn and become aware of considering Bilhah and Zilpah's story?

PUBLIC WITNESS

Because what good are our prayers on Sunday if they make no meaning in our lives on Monday?

Part of our calling as people who claim to follow a God of love, justice, and mercy is to connect what we pray, sing, and hear on Sundays (or the day we set aside to worship God) to the whole of our lives. How does what we pray one day affect where we spend our time and financial resources on another day? How does praying for, about, and with women affect how we vote and who we serve? God's loving call in Deuteronomy 6:5, "You shall love the Lord your God with all your heart, all your soul, and all your strength," commands us to integrate our faith into every aspect of our lives, which includes bearing witness to the good, necessary, and powerful work of justice-seeking, beauty-creating, love-making women in the world today.

Bilhah and Zilpah represent modern-day women, many of them Black and Indigenous, who are often forgotten in our healthcare, justice, and political systems. **Black Women for Wellness** is committed to the health and well-being of Black women and girls through health education, empowerment, and advocacy. **Native Hope** exists to address the injustice done to Native Americans. It does so through sharing stories, providing educational resources, assisting Native communities, and bringing awareness to the fact that across the United States and Canada, Native women and girls are being taken or murdered at unrelenting rates.

Learn more about these organizations. Continue to seek out groups in your own communities that engage work that centers Black and Indigenous women's health and wellbeing, as well as ones that work to end sex trafficking and violence against women and girls of all kinds. Connect. Learn. Give. Grow.[11]

---

[11] McKeever-Burgett, Claire, *Public Witness Woman-Led Nonprofits, https://www.clairemckeeverburgett.com/public-witness, accessed July 10, 2025.*

Part two

Mystics are those who dream dreams and tell the truth, seeing the world both as it is and casting visions for the way it could be; mystics are prophets who are often sought out by men to help discern God's ways, and while there are many women prophets and mystics in the Hebrew Bible (those who give voice to God's commands and who, through surrender and contemplation, seek connection with God), I chose Miriam (and her mother, whom I name Herut), Deborah, Huldah, and Hannah to give voice to feminist interpretations of age-old, male-told stories.

Chapter Five

Miriam and Herut

Liberators | Exodus 2:1–10 and Exodus 15:20–21

Miriam (name): of Hebrew origin meaning "of the sea," "wished-for child," or "bitter"

Herut (name): of Hebrew origin meaning "freedom" or "liberty"

* * *

Now a man from the house of Levi went and married a Levite woman. The woman conceived and bore a son, and when she saw that he was a fine baby, she hid him three months. When she could hide him no longer she got a papyrus basket for him and plastered it with bitumen and pitch; she put the child in it and placed it among the reeds on the bank of the river. His sister stood at a distance, to see what would happen to him.

The daughter of Pharaoh came down to bathe at the river, while her attendants walked beside the river. She saw the basket among the reeds and sent her maid to bring it. When she opened it, she saw the child. He was crying, and she took pity on him. "This must be one of the Hebrews' children," she said. Then his sister said to Pharaoh's daughter, "Shall I go and get you a nurse from the Hebrew women to nurse the child for you?" Pharaoh's daughter said to her, "Yes." So the girl went and called the child's mother. Pharaoh's daughter said to her, "Take this child and nurse it for me, and I will give you your wages." So the woman took the child and nursed it. When the child grew up, she brought him to Pharaoh's daughter, and he became her son. She named him Moses, "because," she said, "I drew him out of the water."

—Exodus 2:1–10

Then the prophet Miriam, Aaron's sister, took a tambourine in her hand, and all the women went out after her with tambourines and with dancing. And Miriam sang to them:

"Sing to the Lord, for he has triumphed gloriously;
horse and rider he has thrown into the sea."

—Exodus 15:20–21

* * *

MIRIAM and HERUT'S STORY

It's not that all babies are born in the dead of night; it's that the birthing mother's body craves the shadows like the desert craves water. It's that when the time comes, whether day or night, she looks for a place to hide to do the work of bringing forth life.

She hides, not because she doesn't want to be seen, but because she knows her work is sacred and personal. She knows that those who are meant to see her will see her and that they too will honor the darkness of the life-giving womb.

Hence, my first job as a midwife is to learn to walk in the dark. To use the senses of touch, smell, and sound to guide me to the mother. When I arrive, my next job is to be present. To observe. To listen. Very few, if any, words are needed; for, so much healing can happen through a simple touch.

Sometimes I rub oil on my hands and then place them on the mother's back. Other times, I lift the lavender to her nose and begin to breathe in through my nose and out through my mouth. The steadier my breathing is, the steadier hers becomes.

By her moans and how she moves through the contractions, I can tell how close she is to pushing. The more constant the moans, the closer we are to meeting the child.

Sometimes, no matter the position, no matter the groans, no matter the wideness of the squat, the baby will not come.

Recalling the times I've witnessed a sheep giving birth to a lamb, its bleating both loud and startling, I begin to mimic the sheep, bleating loudly to startle the baby out of the mama's body. When the birthing process is slow, it's as if the baby is asleep inside its mother, and all it needs is a shrill bleat to shake it from its slumber, reminding it that its one and only job is to move through the birth canal as its mother pushes it to life.

Making noise to bring about life and liberation has been a part of my calling for a very long time.

* * *

From an early age, I felt closest to God when with women. Being the eldest and only daughter born in my family, I spent most of my time in a circle of women. When we weren't giving birth or recovering from giving birth, we were together—telling stories, singing, tending to the flame, preparing meals, and breaking bread.

One of my earliest memories is of a circle of women dancing. There was a fire. It was nighttime. I was supposed to be asleep in the tent. Roused by a steady beat, I awoke. Intrigued by the rhythm, I followed its pulse.

There they were—my grandmothers, my aunties, and my mother, Herut—swaying their hips, stomping their feet, raising their hands and arms to the sky. Some of them even shimmied their shoulders, their breasts shaking from side to side with unabashed abandon. There wasn't a man in sight.

Watching them was like watching the world being made. Both eternal and immediate, their movement drew me closer. I wanted whatever they had.

The next morning, I asked Mama, "Did you sleep well?"

Throwing her head back, she laughed. "I didn't sleep much last night, baby, but it was well."

"What were you doing?" I inquired.

"Making love with the world," she replied.

This is when I knew she'd give birth to my brother, Moses, the deliverer of our people. The only way you can create such a human is by being such a human yourself. Making love with the world, our mama, Herut, knew the only way to be free was to love.

* * *

I was there the day Moses was born. Mama climbed into the birthing cave, and we followed. I bleated like a sheep. Mama moaned. The other women tended and loved. All told, Moses made his way to the earth quickly. Mama pushed a few times and there he was, her son, my brother, our liberator.

I begged her not to let him go. I tried to hide the basket-making supplies. I even clung to her robe like a toddler, hoping I might hold her back from enacting her plan. But she was determined. We were living in an occupied land, and male Hebrew children were being killed left and right.

"What choice do I have, Miriam?" She said my name like a prayer.

"Surely we can think of something else," I cried.

Softening, she took me in her arms and held me close, something she hadn't done in a very long time. My tears soaked her chest, mixing with the leaking milk from her breasts.

"I don't know how, but it will be okay," she said to me, stroking my hair. "I know you love him. I do, too. And it's because of our love for him that we will let him go. It's because of our love for him that he will find freedom and lead others there, too."

So, Mama placed Moses in a basket and sent him floating down the river, hoping someone would find him and take mercy. I stayed close, watching from the reeds. I didn't let that homemade basket leave my sight.

Truth be told, we knew the princess and her maids bathed along that part of the river, and we wanted them to find him, take pity, and enfold him in their care. You don't survive as long as we did without having a plan.

Princess Isis, with her Egyptian name, dark makeup, and stunning wealth, felt the basket graze her back as she rinsed her hair in the water. It was almost as if something or someone moved the basket so it would touch her gently, a soft invitation to turn around and see my baby brother.

As soon as she turned and saw him, she smiled.

Moses began to cry. Still an infant, he was hungry for our mother's milk.

"This must be a Hebrew child," Princess Isis said.

Unafraid, I stepped from behind the reeds, and said, "Shalom. Would you like me to get a Hebrew woman to nurse this child for you?"

"Yes, please," replied the princess.

Running as fast as I could to find our mother, I arrived out of breath and sweaty.

"Mama! Mama!" I yelled.

She emerged from the tent with red eyes and a puffy face. She'd been crying.

"Mama!" I exclaimed again. "The princess found Brother. She wants you to nurse him!"

Mama wasn't as jubilant as I expected her to be. I did not yet know that she would still have to let him go one day. I did not yet know how a mother's heart breaks repeatedly throughout her children's lives, making room for more love and grief, both. I didn't yet know how the heart could contain multitudes.

Still, Mama went to Moses and to the princess, and she cared for her child until he no longer needed her body to survive. Then, with deep sadness that she wore like a blanket for the rest of her life, she took Moses to Princess Isis at the palace, and she said goodbye.

The choice my mother had to make to ensure the survival of our family was not the first time I'd heard of such horror. Living in an occupied land under an oppressive and violent ruler, our people had to make unthinkable decisions and live through unspeakable terrors for years.

However, watching Mama give her son, my brother, away was the first time I had witnessed the atrocity up close. I could hear her heart fracturing, a subtle, small crack that gives way to an avalanche of madness.

Hence, from the moment I watched Mom release Moses into the hands of the oppressor, I became determined to lead our people to freedom.

* * *

"What was it like?" my daughter asks me one night as we stare up at the stars.

"What was *what* like?" I ask in return.

"When you crossed the Red Sea; when the Egyptian army chased you; when you didn't know if you would live or die, but you were willing to find out?"

"Honestly," I reply, "it's like when a mother begins the work of giving birth. She can't *not* do it. Her body moves her in ways that her mind may not understand. Having lived in such terror for so long, we couldn't *not* leave. Our bodies told us, 'It's time.' Thankfully, we followed."

"Were you afraid?" my daughter asks.

"Hell, yes!" I exclaim.

"How did you do it?" My precious girl is deeply perplexed by our people's journey, and I love her for her curiosity and care.

"We stomped and moaned and sang and breathed our way out of Egypt," I say. "As for the sea swallowing the soldiers, that's between them and God."

"Sing me the song you sang, Mama," she beckons as she lays her head in my lap.

I begin to hum the tune about Mother God of shore and sea, setting Her people free as she falls asleep in my lap. Remembering the multitudes of miles I crossed to get here, where I rest, even if only for a moment under the forever sky with my daughter, is a dream come true.

I loved and still love Moses with all my heart. I prophesied his birth; I helped save his life. And? I love our mother more. I joined Moses to lead our people to the promised land because of her. Her witness, her sacrifice, her fierceness, her love.

I'm not sure Moses ever knew this to be my motivation and truth, but I trust he'll soon find out when he meets Mama on the other side, and, with love and honesty, she whispers in his ear, "Your sister, the women, and I are the liberators. You freed others because we first freed you."

I imagine he'll nod his head, finally knowing the truth, and I pray that it won't take dying for the rest of us to see and know the power, love, and freedom-making of women.

* * *

To my mother, Herut, love-maker and freedom fighter, I thank you, and I love you. Forever and for always. Amen.

LITURGY FOR MORNING PRAYER

If you are gathered with others, position yourselves in a circle. Place a lit candle in the center, or, if you're feeling adventurous, make a fire, and practice this liturgy outside, forming a circle around it. If you are alone, light a candle (or make a fire) as a sign of connection to Mother God and the circle of women who join you, even here, even now, as you pray.

Opening Prayer

God, who is our Mother and who is blessedly beyond all names and identities that we can imagine, Your love is lavish. From sunrise to sunset, from moonrise to moonset, your mothering embrace wraps us up in your mercy, and we are abundantly grateful. So also, we, by your grace, offer love, mercy, and gratitude. Amen.

Psalm 136: 1–9 (inspired by the *New Revised Standard Version* of the Bible)

Give thanks to God, for She is like a mother,

Steadfast in love, enduring in presence, and faithful to her children.

Give thanks to God, for She is like a mother,
Creating new worlds, teaching us to play, standing up to injustice.

Give thanks to God, for She is like a mother,

Making all things new, by Her grace, by Her mercy.

Give thanks to God, for She is like a mother,

Weaving baskets of safety and forging ways where there aren't any.

Give thanks to God, for She is like a mother,

Giving birth in the sacred waters that soften their way through our sometimes-tortured lives.

Give thanks to God, for She is like a mother,

Casting visions of light and finding shadows in which to rest.

Give thanks to God, for She is like a mother,

Dancing on the shores of victory, leading Her loved ones home.

Scripture Reading: Exodus 2:1–10 and Exodus 15:20–21

A living, breathing Word.

Thanks be to Mother God.

Hold several moments of quiet for prayer and reflection.

Prayers of the People

In peace, let us pray…

Have mercy

For a world in which lands and people are not things to occupy but sacred blessings to love…

May it be so.

For a world in which calling God Mother is not scandalous or edgy but holy and true…

May it be so.

For a world in which no one is oppressed by violence and greed…

May it be so.

For a world in which every one of us is free because nobody's free until everybody's free[12]...

May it be so.

For a world in which the brokenhearted are comforted and the comfortable are brokenhearted...

May it be so.

For a world in which women dance for themselves and their joy, first and foremost...

May it be so.

For a world in which we do not have to die to know the truth...

May it be so.

For a world in which the hungry are fed and the unhoused are sheltered and the sick are healed...

May it be so.

For a world in which women and girls do not fear for their lives...

May it be so.

For a world in which giving birth is treated as holy and sacred ...

May it be so.

By Your love, may our prayers be answered as you work in us and through us...

[Moment of silence for additional prayers from your heart to the Heart of God.]

In the communion of God, our Mother,

Wisdom, our Sister, and

Spirit, our Daughter,

---

[12] Fannie Lou Hamer, an American voting and women's rights activist, community organizer, and leader of the Civil Rights Movement, said "Nobody's free until everybody's free" in a speech delivered at the founding of the National Women's Political Caucus in Washington, D.C., on July 10, 1971. She used this phrase to emphasize the interconnectedness of freedom and the need for collective liberation for all people, something we still must pray for and proclaim today.

We entrust ourselves to You and Your mercy.

May it be so. Amen.

Song of Praise

Contemporary Connection

Take a few moments to watch and listen to "Free," by Florence and the Machine.[13] *Imagine Miriam and her mother, Herut, along with the other women in their family and community singing and dancing this together as they stare at the stars, reunited around a fire, in the land of love. Invite this song to be a part of your prayerful, worshipful, songful life.*

The Prayer of the Women

Holy Mother of sand and sea,

to You all honor and praise.

When we cry out, You hear us.

When we ask for help, You help us.

When we long to be loved, You love us.

May mercy be offered to everyone.

---

[13] McKeever-Burgett, Claire, *Music for Contemporary Connections,* https://www.clairemckeeverburgett.com/*music, accessed July 10, 2025.*

May power and dominion over others cease.
May greed and violence end.
May love live forever.
Birth us into a new world.
Help us make this one beautiful.
Stir us up. Settle us down.
Burn. Simmer. Refine.
When all else shakes, hold us steady.
When everyone else wants to blame,
remind us that in You there is only Love.
Our praise and our prayers are Yours, forever. Amen.

Closing Blessing

May you know love.
May you know Mother God.
May you know powerful women.
May you witness the birth of new life
and new worlds, again and again,
as we go from this time and this place,
creating alongside Mother God
a liberated and liberating world for everyone.
Amen.

REFLECTION QUESTIONS

The following questions are meant to deepen and expand, invite and beckon thoughtful, compassionate, and curious responses to the story and liturgy of Miriam and Herut. Whether considering these questions on your own or in a group setting, create space for journaling, collaging, or painting in response. If engaging in group discussion, choose one or two questions, at most, to hold at the center of your sacred circle.

1. In what ways do you connect with Miriam and Herut's story? What feels redemptive? What feels challenging?
2. When reading and praying with Miriam and Herut, Mother God, and the women, what sensations do you notice in your body?
3. From what (or whom) do you need to be liberated? What does freedom look like to you?
4. With whom and what might God be inviting you to spend time and learn considering Miriam and Herut's story?

PUBLIC WITNESS

Because what good are our prayers on Sunday if they make no meaning in our lives on Monday?

Part of our calling as people who claim to follow a God of love, justice, and mercy is to connect what we pray, sing, and hear on Sundays (or the day we set aside to worship God) to the whole of our lives. How does what we pray one day affect where we spend our time and financial resources on another day? How does praying for, about, and with women affect how we vote and who we serve? God's loving call in Deuteronomy 6:5, "You shall love the Lord your God with all your heart, all your soul, and all your strength," commands us to integrate our faith into every aspect of our lives, which includes bearing witness to the good, necessary, and powerful work of justice-seeking, beauty-creating, love-making women in the world today.

Miriam and Herut, like Bilhah and Zilpah and many other women in our sacred scriptures, represent modern-day women, many of them Black and Indigenous, who are often forgotten in our healthcare, justice, and political systems. **Black Women's Health Imperative** offers national programs in health policy, education, research, knowledge and leadership development, and communications to save and extend the lives of Black women. **National Indigenous Women's Resource Center** provides national leadership to end violence against American Indian, Alaska Native, and Native Hawaiian women by lifting the collective voices of grassroots advocates and offering culturally grounded resources, technical assistance and training, and policy development to strengthen tribal sovereignty.

Learn more about these organizations. Continue to seek out groups in your own communities that center Black and Indigenous women and the issues facing them. Connect. Learn. Give. Grow.[14]

---

[14] McKeever-Burgett, Claire, *Public Witness Woman-Led Nonprofits, https://www.clairemckeeverburgett.com/public-witness, accessed July 10, 2025.*

Chapter Six

Deborah

Songmaker | Judges 4 and 5

Deborah, woman of Lappidoth (name): of Hebrew origin meaning "woman of torches"

* * *

At that time Deborah, a prophetess, wife of Lappidoth, was judging Israel. She used to sit under the palm of Deborah between Ramah and Bethel in the hill country of Ephraim; and the Israelites came up to her for judgment.

—Judges 4:4–5

Then Deborah and Barak sang on that day...

—Judges 5:1

* * *

DEBORAH'S STORY

I sit below a palm tree, cooled by its shade. One by one, they come, a long line of people seeking women's wisdom.

How do we defeat the Canaanites? What is the meaning of life? How do I settle the dispute with my brother? What is right? What is wrong?

In response, I sing songs and tell tales, spinning words and melodies together. The answers to their questions are not for the faint of heart nor are they the plainspoken simplicity for which they long.

Instead, the answers dance in the air, eluding right, evading wrong. I am merely the one invited to dance alongside the flame and to relay what I hear and see burning at its center.

I am the woman of torches. Here not to tame the fire but to stoke it.

My song is one of the oldest of its kind, surviving year after year, war after war, ruler after ruler. My voice can still be heard echoing across valleys:

Awake! Awake! Arise! Arise!

Be a friend of the fire.

Turn your face toward the sun.

A refrain, an invitation, to seek that which burns, not to destroy, but to refine. A refrain, an invitation of, by, from, and about the women.

Tell me: how often have you heard stories of the battlefields from the perspective of women? How often have you seen the fighting through our eyes and imagined the leading coming from us? We were there, too, laying our lives on the line. We were there, too, trying to end the war. We were there, too, tending the injured and feeding the hungry. We were there, too, singing, singing, singing.

The divine feminine, who lives within us all, fights the enemy, not with weapons but with melodies, not with starvation but with food, not with hate but with love.

In Judges 5, you can read my song as told *by* men and *for* men. Here, you can read my song as told from my perspective—not theirs. Though my song is millennia old, it offers each of us an invitation into a life that burns with justice, kindness, nuance, and love. Its melody, joined by the harmonies of other women truth-tellers, heeds an ancient call to awaken, arise, befriend, and turn. My song, my voice, our song, our voices, sing. Are you listening?

We walk the streets with long hair, wild and untied.

Kings and princes, rulers and lords listen to our songs.

For we sing truth, we judge honestly, we see clearly.

I am Deborah, a mother in Israel, a prophet among prophets, a judge among judges, my wisdom comes from women who've encircled me from the very beginning. Warriors and peacemakers, mothers and maidens, hunters and gatherers. All of us together, all of us holy.

When the clouds unleashed their water, when the mountains shook before Yahweh, we were there.

When new gods were chosen, when war tore apart the lands, we bore witness.

When rulers rode on white donkeys and squandered their money on rich carpets, ignoring the poor, we held vigil.

We marched with the marchers; we gathered with the gatherers.

From Ephraim to Machir to Zebulun to Issachar to Naphtali, we beckoned:

Awake! Awake!

Arise! Arise!

Be a friend of the fire.

Turn your face toward the sun.

They heard the call. They came.

But they demanded eyes for eyes and death for death. It was the only way they knew.

Only into the hands of a woman will the enemy be delivered, we said.

Why is that? They inquired.

Look at us, we replied, are we not the very water from the sky? The very flame of the fire? The very source of God? Did Jael not drive a tent peg into Sisera's head, defending herself, and in so doing, defending threatened women everywhere?

Echoing Barak to Deborah, they said, "If the women go, we will follow."

The women went, Deborah at the lead. Enemies and fears were washed away. Violence and evil died in a woman's arms.

In a land far away, Sisera's mother sat at the window, watching and waiting for her son to arrive. The longer and longer she waited, the more she grieved.

Even though she knew the ills of her son, even though she disagreed with everything he had been taught, everything he had inherited, everything he had justified and enacted, his actions made him no less her son—blood of her blood, bone of her bone, flesh of her flesh.

Women who were not our own were still ours; therefore, we refused to leave Sisera's mother and sisters to the death and destruction of men, even men we called our relatives.

The wisest among us rescued, protected, saved. The wisest among us proclaimed:

> *Awake! Awake!*
>
> *Arise! Arise!*
>
> *Be a friend of the fire.*
>
> *Turn your face toward the sun.*

The land rested for forty years, not because we dominated and destroyed it, but because we collaborated with and cared for it.

We awoke. We arose. We befriended. We turned.

I, Deborah, leading the way with the women above, beside, below, and behind me, singing:

> *Awake! Awake!*
>
> *Arise! Arise!*
>
> *Be a friend of the fire.*
>
> *Turn your face toward the sun.*

LITURGY FOR MIDDAY PRAYER

OPENING

If you are gathered with others, position yourselves in a circle. Place a lit candle in the center. If you are alone, light a candle as a sign of connection to the circle of women who join you, even now, as you pray. As an alternative to lighting a candle, if the weather is conducive, consider observing midday prayer outside with your face turned toward the sun. Either way, anyway, trust the warmth of God and the women to be with you and in you, even here, even now, as you pray.

Call to Prayer

Awake! Awake! Arise! Arise!
Be a friend of the fire. Turn your face toward the sun.

Prayer at Midday

God of the noonday sun that warms us even when we cannot see it or feel it, thank you for this moment of rest that reminds us of the fiery flame you seek to tend in us and among us. Where we need inspiration, awaken us to your love. Where we need patience, awaken us to your steady hand. Remind us that the work of justice is long and that you are with us every step of the way. May our work be warm, our hearts be kind, and our lives be whole in You. Amen.

Psalm 68

As smoke rises from the flame,
so God rises to meet us in our fear and uncertainty.
Melting away our need to conquer and prevail,
God, the fire, refines us in and through love.
We rejoice in gladness, not because others die,
but because we live to see the glory of God who saves all.
So we sing the song of Deborah and of the women
who tell of God's faithfulness and freedom.
We sing of the women who care for the poor,
protect others, and embody the goodness of our God.
First, the singers sing.
Then, the musicians play.
Led by young women, banging on drums.

Bless the God of fire,
Bless the God of love.
Sing, Sing, Sing.

Scripture Reading: Judges 5

A living, breathing Word.

Thanks be to Mother God.

Hold several moments of quiet for prayer and reflection.

Song of Praise

Contemporary Connection

Take a few moments to watch and listen to "I'm on Fire" by The Staves and "Fly" by Anna Graves.[15] *Imagine Deborah singing these songs with a community of women tending a fire. Invite these songs into your prayerful, worshipful, songful life.*

The Prayer of the Women

Holy Mother of sand and sea,

to You all honor and praise.

[15] McKeever-Burgett, Claire, *Music for Contemporary Connections,* https://www.clairemckeeverburgett.com/*music, accessed July 10, 2025.*

When we cry out, You hear us.

When we ask for help, You help us.

When we long to be loved, You love us.

May mercy be offered to everyone.

May power and dominion over others cease.

May greed and violence end.

May love live forever.

Birth us into a new world.

Help us make this one beautiful.

Stir us up. Settle us down.

Burn. Simmer. Refine.

When all else shakes, hold us steady.

When everyone else wants to blame,

remind us that in You there is only Love.

Our praise and our prayers are Yours, forever. Amen.

Closing Blessing

As we leave this place, set our hearts on fire, Mother God,

that we may live and serve in Your gracious, abundant,
forever love. **Amen.**

REFLECTION QUESTIONS

The following questions are meant to deepen and expand, invite and beckon thoughtful, compassionate, and curious responses to the story and liturgy of Deborah. Whether considering these questions on your own or in a group setting, create space for journaling, collaging, or painting in response. If engaging in group discussion, choose one or two questions, at most, to hold at the center of your sacred circle.

1. What resonates with you about Deborah's story? What feels redemptive? What feels challenging?
2. When reading and praying with Deborah, Mother God, and the women, what sensations do you notice in your body?

3. What women leaders do you follow and why?
4. If you were to write a short song, what would the song say?
5. Recall a time when music played a role in your life. Consider sharing it with the group. If you're alone, consider writing about it.

PUBLIC WITNESS

Because what good are our prayers on Sunday if they make no meaning in our lives on Monday?

Part of our calling as people who claim to follow a God of love, justice, and mercy is to connect what we pray, sing, and hear on Sundays (or the day we set aside to worship God) to the whole of our lives. How does what we pray one day affect where we spend our time and financial resources on another day? How does praying for, about, and with women affect how we vote and whom we serve? God's loving call in Deuteronomy 6:5, "You shall love the Lord your God with all your heart, all your soul, and all your strength," commands us to integrate our faith into every aspect of our lives, which includes bearing witness to the good, necessary, and powerful work of justice-seeking, beauty-creating, love-making women in the world today.

Deborah and the women with whom she keeps company and tends the fire (as I've imagined them) are the kind of leaders I want in all places where decisions are being made. **Women in Leadership** seeks to accelerate women's full and effective participation in leadership at all levels of decision-making in economic and public life, particularly in the fields of health, law, and economics. **Her Bold Move** supports candidates from every corner of the United States running for seats up and down the ballot. As they work to shatter glass ceilings, they target seats that have never been held by a woman at any point in history. Their plan is critical and unapologetic: They focus their efforts on women running for offices in states with abortion bans, which are the same states with the lowest numbers of women in government. Their work chips away at the male supermajorities in these chambers to ensure women are in all places where decisions are being made. I can imagine Deborah working with and supporting these organizations in myriad ways, and I can imagine her encouraging you to do the same.

Learn more about these organizations. Continue to support groups in your own communities that promote women's leadership in all places where decisions are being made. Connect. Learn. Give. Grow.[16]

---

[16] McKeever-Burgett, Claire, *Public Witness Woman-Led Nonprofits, https://www.clairemckeeverburgett.com/public-witness, accessed July 10, 2025.*

Chapter Seven

Huldah

Visionary | 2 Kings 22:14–20

Huldah (name): of Hebrew origin meaning "mole"

* * *

So the priest Hilkiah, Ahikam, Achbor, Shaphan, and Asaiah went to the prophet Huldah the wife of Shallum son of Tikvah son of Harhas, keeper of the wardrobe; she resided in Jerusalem in the Second Quarter, where they consulted her. She declared to them, "Thus says the Lord, the God of Israel: Tell the man who sent you to me: 'Thus says the Lord: I will indeed bring disaster on this place and on its inhabitants—all the words of the book that the king of Judah has read. Because they have abandoned me and have made offerings to other gods, so that they have provoked me to anger with all the work of their hands, therefore my wrath will be kindled against this place, and it will not be quenched.' But as to the king of Judah who sent you to inquire of the Lord, thus shall you say to him: 'Thus says the Lord, the God of Israel: Regarding the words that you have heard, because your heart was penitent and you humbled yourself before the Lord, when you heard how I spoke against this place and against its inhabitants, that they should become a desolation and a curse, and because you have torn your clothes and wept before me, I also have heard you, says the Lord. Therefore, I will gather you to your ancestors, and you shall be gathered to your grave in peace; your eyes shall not see all the disaster that I will bring on this place.'" They took the message back to the king.

—2 Kings 22:14–20

* * *

HULDAH'S STORY

From the time of my youth, I could hear God speaking to me. Sometimes Her voice sounded like a bird's song. At other times, it moved like rushing water over smooth rocks after a rainfall. It was the rumble of thunder. The crack of lightning. The swish of trees blowing in the wind. God spoke in whispers. God spoke in wails.

In ways I cannot explain, only accept and channel, God's voice was like hearing everything and nothing all at once. As a paradox and a puzzle, God both burned and blessed my ears and my heart.

* * *

Because my family was wealthy, I could read and write by the age of five. I buried myself in ancient scrolls and surrounded myself with wise teachers, reading closely, listening carefully. Like the small, burrowing animal for which I was named, I crawled into the teachings of old, allowing them to become my home.

While it was rare for most women to become scholars, I was not most women. Not only was my family wealthy, I also married Shallum, keeper of the royal wardrobe, at the age of eighteen. Shallum's occupation enabled us to live in the palace, so my social status and proximity to royalty gave me easy access to academic life.

Furthermore, God implored me to learn. In all Her infinite sagacity, She said, "Listen and learn. And share what you learn with the people."

See, the God who spoke to me and in me and through me wasn't interested in keeping knowledge hidden or inaccessible to others. Rather, the God who spoke to me and in me and through me wanted the truth shared widely because, as She would often say, "The truth will set you free."

* * *

Early each morning, I arise before the sun and make my way to a gate along the outer palace wall, known as Huldah's Gate. People visit me with questions and curiosities about everything from, "How did we get here?" to "Who are we?" to "What do God's promises to our ancestors mean for us today?"

I listen closely and then share a poem or a prayer in response. It is a way to offer a faithful reply without pretending to know the answer outright. Life is a mystery, after all, and we are wise to embrace it as such. We women know intuitively what men often spend years trying to discover. It's not that we are born this way; it's that our intuition is often what keeps us safe and alive, cultivated through years of necessity. Many of the men I know seek the answers outside of themselves, so they come to me begging for answers, longing for exhortations. At every turn, I try to channel God's voice through my own, pointing them back to themselves. It is the way of women's wisdom to say repeatedly: *The answers are within you because that's where God lives.*

Often, though, the wisdom I share falls on closed ears. Instead of looking within, many create altars to worship gods other than Adonai.[17] They forget who and whose they are. They act as if the Source of Life hasn't saved them a thousand times over. They live convinced that the answers are elsewhere.

* * *

It was like any other day when I received the call from King Josiah. I was dressed in a purple robe, sitting on the steps at the gate.

"Huldah," the messenger said. "King Josiah has summoned you."

Though the King and Shallum were close colleagues, I was rarely summoned into the King's company without my husband present. Still, something within told me I needed to go.

"Take me to him," I said to the messenger.

When I arrived in the King's library, Josiah and a group of men were bent over a fray-edged scroll, which was open on the table before them.

"Your majesty," said the messenger. "I bring you Huldah."

The group of men looked up, surveying every inch of my body with their eyes. One of them sneered. Another laughed. I pressed my

[17] Hebrew meaning for Lord.

shoulders back and lifted my chin. Their disdain would not intimidate me. I'd dealt with greater men before.

King Josiah stepped from behind the cedar surface. "Huldah," he said. "Welcome."

I offered a subtle bow in his direction, but kept my eyes raised. Groups of men made me uneasy with their smug yet fragile sense of power.

"Excuse their lack of respect," the King said. "It's just that we've discovered a scroll and are trying to understand it. Currently, it has us vexed."

"And of what concern is this to me?" I asked.

"You are an academic and a scholar," the King said, "someone who's been interpreting the Law and channeling God's voice for years now. I know you sit at a palace gate. I know people come to you for answers. I come to you now asking for the same."

"While it would be an honor to help, my King, I do not interpret on demand. I will need time with the scroll. I will need solitude with God. I will need space to breathe."

"Your wish is my command," replied the King. "Gentlemen," he said, "Leave."

The men huffed and puffed their way out of the room, leaving me alone before the table, the scroll, and God.

Before the King left, though, he turned to me with one last question.

"What makes you so bold?" he asked. "I don't know many women like you."

"Interesting," I replied. "I hope you'll get to know more of us. We are everywhere."

"Huh," King Josiah cocked his head, amused and intrigued.

"I hope you hear God's voice today," said the King. "I'll leave a messenger outside the door for when you are ready to call me."

With that, the king left me alone with the scroll.

* * *

Poring over the words before me, I soon realized that they were remnants from the Torah and that their message might be difficult to hear. Hashem[18] always had a way of being clear about what was required of Hashem's people; Yahweh's people had always had a way of confusing Hashem's commands.

Before writing a summary of the scrolls' meaning, I sank to the ground, crossing my legs, resting my hands, palms open on my knees.

"Holy Source of All Being who's been speaking to me and in me and through me forever," I prayed, "What am I to make of your words? What am I to make of this Law? Who are you, and who are we in relation to you?"

It was quiet for a long time before I heard the Almighty whisper:

> *I am Love. I do not destroy or punish. The people do that to themselves. I long for all to seek and serve Love, which always restores and always saves. Remember, beloved, I often bear the blame of others' actions. I often am created in others' images. Whoever gets to tell the story, whoever gets to interpret the Law are the ones who get to tell and interpret me. However, like I once told Moses, "I am who I am." A verb. An action.*
> *Love.*

God's words hung in the air like the smoke from the burning candles. I breathed them in. I held them close.

Looking down at the palms of my hands, I saw the words resting there, waiting for me to gather them up and bring them to my heart, waiting for me to act.

Pressing my hands into the earth, I stood. Taking a quill and parchment, I wrote the meaning of the words on the scroll for the messenger to deliver to King Josiah:

> *This is what the LORD, the God of Israel, says: Tell the man who sent you to me, "This is what the LORD says: Disaster will fall on this place and its people, according to everything written in the book the king of Judah has read. Because they have forsaken Love and burned away the truth, they will suffer."*
>
> *But tell the man who sent you to me, "Because your heart was responsive and you humbled yourself before Love and because you*

[18] Hebrew for "The Name."

> *tore your robes and wept in God's presence, your ancestors will greet you and you will die in peace. All who humble themselves to Love will know peace."*

* * *

Many people chose to ignore Love and Her commands. They turned aside from Her teachings, forsaking the Holy One's instructions to care for the poor, feed the hungry, heal the sick, and listen to wisdom.

It was true what God said: it wasn't God who brought disaster upon them. Suffering was not ordained by the Holy; it was humans who allowed it, who chose it, who often created it. Calamity and chaos could have been avoided if only the people had listened and loved.

* * *

For years, I sat at the palace gate. For years, I shared foresight and prophecy. For years, I preached the same sermon every day. Plain and simple, "Follow Love, and Her ways will heal you. Follow Love, and you will die in peace."

Sometimes they listened. Sometimes they didn't. It was up to me to discern Love's wisdom and to share it, but I could not make others' choices for them. I knew, like I knew when I was young, that I was to listen, I was to love, and that God would take care of the rest.

* * *

I died not knowing the end of my people's story. Perhaps that's because their story is still unfolding. After all, the love story between God and God's people still takes shape today. They say that if it weren't for me and my intelligence the story may have ended; they marveled at all those powerful men listening to a woman; they tried to write Love and me out of the story altogether.

But we women, like Love, persist. We burrow in, digging deep into the heart of the matter, taking curved and slanted paths to the truth, if necessary, dogged in our belief that Love cannot be erased if it lives in and through us.

Like a bird's song, a rush of water over slick rocks after a rainstorm, a rumble of thunder, a crack of lightning, a swish of trees blowing in the wind, a whisper, a wail, God speaks; we are wise to listen, and the world is wise to hear us singing an anthem of love.

LITURGY FOR MORNING PRAYER

OPENING

If you are gathered with others, position yourselves in a circle. Place a lit candle in the center. If you are alone, light a candle as a sign of connection to Mother God and to the circle of women who join you, even here, even now, as you pray.

Morning Wisdom

God who is love renews our strength from day to day.

God who is love speaks truth to our inner beings.

God who is love shows us what is good: doing justice, loving mercy, walking humbly.

Amen.

Morning Prayer

Holy One, who speaks through the prophet Huldah, help us listen to your words, help us move with your actions, help us act in accordance with your love. Amen.

Morning Psalm | Psalm 107

Give thanks to God; Her love endures forever.

We, God's redeemed, confess that when we allow the power of our fears to lead us, God saves us.

Give thanks to God; Her love endures forever.

We, God's redeemed, confess that when we wander into wastelands of defensiveness and despair, God delivers us.

Give thanks to God; Her love endures forever.

We, God's redeemed, confess that when we try to fill ourselves with things other than God's love, God rescues us.

Give thanks to God; Her love endures forever.

We, God's redeemed, confess that when we seek the pits of doom and follow the way of contempt, God turns our faces toward light and forgiveness.

Give thanks to God; Her love endures forever.

We, God's redeemed, contemplate the loving acts of God, seeking wisdom, enacting mercy, living love.

Give thanks to God; Her love endures forever.

Amen.

Scripture Reading: 2 Kings 22:14–20

A living, breathing Word.

Thanks be to Mother God.

Hold several moments of quiet for prayer and reflection.

Prayers of the People

Our prayers today are guided through meditative questions that seek to turn us inward in order that we may engage the world, centered in God and full of love. Find a comfortable place to sit, with both feet on the ground, and shoulders softened away from the ears. Find breath—in through the nose, out through the mouth. Close your eyes, if that feels safe, or simply gaze forward softly. As you breathe, in and out, in and out, consider the following:

What does a loving God look like? How does a loving God act?

[Hold space for quiet breathing, praying, and reflection.]

What images of God need to fall away to know love more deeply?

[Hold space for quiet breathing, praying, and reflection.]

What does a softened mind, body, heart, and spirit look like and feel like?

[Hold space for quiet breathing, praying, and reflection.]

Who are you being called to love through service and action?

[Hold space for quiet breathing, praying, and reflection.]

Holy God of this time, Holy God of all times, hear our prayers and hold them in Your gracious Love, we pray. Amen.

Song of Praise

In the Beginning

Claire K. McKeever-Burgett

Contemporary Connection

Take a few moments to watch and listen to "Superwoman" by Alicia Keys.[19] *Imagine Huldah singing this at Huldah's Gate, inviting all women to sing it along with her. Sing it to yourself and to the women in your life who keep you grounded in love. Invite this song into your prayerful, worshipful, songful life.*

The Prayer of the Women

Holy Mother of sand and sea,
to You all honor and praise.
When we cry out, You hear us.
When we ask for help, You help us.
When we long to be loved, You love us.
May mercy be offered to everyone.

---

[19] McKeever-Burgett, Claire, *Music for Contemporary Connections,* https://www.clairemckeeverburgett.com/*music, accessed July 10, 2025.*

May power and dominion over others cease.

May greed and violence end.

May love live forever.

Birth us into a new world.

Help us make this one beautiful.

Stir us up. Settle us down.

Burn. Simmer. Refine.

When all else shakes, hold us steady.

When everyone else wants to blame,

remind us that in You there is only Love.

Our praise and our prayers are Yours, forever. Amen.

Blessing and Sending Forth

Holy Mother God,

Help us listen. Help us love. Amen.

REFLECTION QUESTIONS

The following questions are meant to deepen and expand, invite and beckon thoughtful, compassionate, and curious responses to the story and liturgy of Huldah. Whether considering these questions on your own or in a group setting, create space for journaling, collaging, or painting in response. If engaging in group discussion, choose one or two questions, at most, to hold at the center of your sacred circle.

1. What resonates with you about Huldah's story? What feels redemptive? What feels challenging?
2. When reading and praying along with Huldah, Mother God, and the women, what sensations do you notice in your body?
3. What stories or ideas do you have about women that might change if you heard them tell their story in their own words?
4. What is your story? What do you want your story to be?
5. What is your story about God? What do you want your story about God to be?

PUBLIC WITNESS

Because what good are our prayers on Sunday if they make no meaning in our lives on Monday?

Part of our calling as people who claim to follow a God of love, justice, and mercy is to connect what we pray, sing, and hear on Sundays (or the day we set aside to worship God) to the whole of our lives. How does what we pray one day affect where we spend our time and financial resources on another day? How does praying for, about, and with women affect how we vote and whom we serve? God's loving call in Deuteronomy 6:5, "You shall love the Lord your God with all your heart, all your soul, and all your strength," commands us to integrate our faith into every aspect of our lives, which includes bearing witness to the good, necessary, and powerful work of justice-seeking, beauty-creating, love-making women in the world today.

Huldah, the interpreting woman, begs us through her life and witness to ensure that all women and girls have access to education so they can make informed, empowered decisions about their lives. The **Malala Fund** focuses on accelerating progress—challenging systems, policies, and practices so that all girls can access twelve years of free, safe, quality education, no matter where they live or who they are. **The Representation Project** awakens consciousness of intersectional gender stereotypes through film, education, and activism and invites everyone to build a more equitable future for all.

Learn more about these organizations. Continue to support groups in your own communities that promote girls' and women's education, as well as the upending of intersectional gender stereotypes everywhere. Connect. Learn. Give. Grow.[20]

---

[20] McKeever-Burgett, Claire, *Public Witness Woman-Led Nonprofits, https://www.clairemckeeverburgett.com/public-witness, accessed July 10, 2025.*

Chapter Eight

Hannah

Seeker | 1 Samuel 1:2, 9–16; 2:1–10

Hannah (name): of Hebrew origin meaning "grace" or "favor"

* * *

He had two wives; the name of one was Hannah, and the name of the other Peninnah. Peninnah had children, but Hannah had no children.

—1 Samuel 1:2

After they had eaten and drunk at Shiloh, Hannah rose and presented herself before the Lord. Now Eli the priest was sitting on the seat beside the doorpost of the temple of the Lord. She was deeply distressed and prayed to the Lord and wept bitterly. She made this vow: "O Lord of hosts, if only you will look on the misery of your servant and remember me and not forget your servant but will give to your servant a male child, then I will set him before you as a nazirite until the day of his death. He shall drink neither wine nor intoxicants, and no razor shall touch his head."

As she continued praying before the Lord, Eli observed her mouth. Hannah was praying silently; only her lips moved, but her voice was not heard; therefore Eli thought she was drunk. So Eli said to her, "How long will you make a drunken spectacle of yourself? Put away your wine." But Hannah answered, "No, my lord, I am a woman deeply troubled; I have drunk neither wine nor strong drink, but I have been pouring out my soul before the Lord. Do not regard your servant as a worthless woman, for I have been speaking out of my great anxiety and vexation all this time."

—1 Samuel 1:9–16

Hannah prayed and said,

"My heart exults in the Lord;
my strength is exalted in my God.
My mouth derides my enemies,
because I rejoice in my victory..."

—1 Samuel 2:1

* * *

HANNAH'S STORY

My body is wrecked with sobbing. I cannot stop, which is why I never wanted to begin in the first place. But these waves were always coming, and I always knew I'd be powerless when they arrived.

I fold at the waist and fall to my knees. The dry dirt sinks into the cracks of my skin, mixing with the wet of my sweating, weeping body.

There's a small altar I made from cedar and sage in front of me. Though I know God is everywhere, it helps to have something to see and touch when I'm weak and wrecked. With no more pretense, every truth laid bare, I hope to God the cedar and sage can take what I'm laying down.

Moving the back of my hand across my upper lip, I make a feeble attempt to wipe the snot dripping from my nose.

"Why," I wail at the void, the sky, the wind, the wood.

"Why am I not pregnant?" I scream.

I rock back and forth. I clutch my chest. It hurts so bad.

"What have I done wrong?" I spit. "I'll do anything to have a child! Anything!"

The bread and wine I've stopped consuming to try to make myself pregnant taunt me at every turn. I watch the men eat and drink whatever they want, and I want to rip their tongues from their bodies. Sabbath is no longer Sabbath to me. Rest, relaxation, and renewal are distant dreams.

It's not fair, I think as my heart hardens just a little bit more.

I mix the herbs with hot water like the midwives instruct. I sleep on my side. I try new positions when Elkanah and I make love. I lift my hips to the air afterward to help his seed grow within me.

"So, you tell me, oh Powerful One, oh God Almighty who sits on a throne, what can I do to make this right? What sins am I to atone? What wrong am I to make right?"

Short of breath, I pause and reach my forehead to the earth. My legs stretch long behind me. I am now belly down, face down, lying in the dirt like a snake, crying, snorting, gasping, hitting.

After a while, I am too tired to move. The tears, no longer a fountain, but a slow drip. My fists hurt too much to hit the ground one more time. I inhaled enough dirt while wallowing on the earth to make myself cough blood, so my body offers me a reprieve. She stops.

In the stillness, I hear a soft scratch of someone's feet upon the earth. They move toward me. Then, I feel someone breathing.

"Who is it?" I ask without lifting my head or opening my eyes.

"It's Penninah," a soft voice replies.

She's the last person I want to see; the second wife of my husband, Elkanah. The one who gave him a male son on demand, or so it seemed. Her very existence haunts me.

"What do you want?" I ask.

"I couldn't help but hear you," she says. "I want to be near you in your pain."

I'm too tired to tell her to leave so I remain motionless in my dust bed. Turning my head to the left, I close my eyes and breathe.

After a pregnant pause, she speaks. "I know you feel like this is all your fault," she says quietly, almost whispering. "I know you think that if you did something different or better, you might be pregnant by now. I know you carry the weight of your world's, your religion's, your family's and your own expectations on your shoulders. I know you think it's all up to you."

"But it's not," she says. "I don't know a lot, but I know that not even God can make a person pregnant or not. If God could—make us pregnant or not pregnant—what kind of God would that be? A giant asshole, if you ask me."

Penninah calling God an asshole gets me to smile a half grin that curves up the side of my face.

"What if it's not your fault, Hannah? What if God is with all of us, no matter what? What if it's not all about getting pregnant and having male sons? What if we could let go of the false notion that we're responsible for everything?"

I am like a root, buried and growing deep. Her words hang in the air, refusing to blow away with the wind.

Salty tears move down the side of my cheek. My staccato breath gets caught in my throat as I try to suppress a sob.

I cannot bear to look at her. That's the thing with the truth—it's hard to hear and even harder to see.

Before she leaves, she places her hand on the side of my face, wipes my tears, and then walks away.

* * *

Shaming childless women is a tale as old as time. Growing up, the only women without children were the ones whispered about behind closed doors.

She's a witch. She doesn't want them. She's being punished for her sins.

Therefore, I grew up fearing childlessness. I heard what was said about women with no children, particularly those with no *male* children, and I did not want those things said about me, nor did I want the reality of their plight.

"Mama, what do I need to do to make sure I have a child?" I asked when I was ten.

"Pray to God," Mama replied. "Like the meaning of your name, beg for God's mercy and favor to be upon you."

So, I did as I was told. Day and night, I prayed for a child. Long before I was married to Elkanah ("E" as he affectionately became known to me), I implored God, "Make me a mother."

With motherhood as the highest currency for women, I understood it as my fulfillment of my God-made design to bear, birth, and raise male heirs to keep the lineage growing. I acted as if my body was only here for one purpose and one purpose alone—to grow and give my husband and the world a male child.

Though I shudder at these outdated ideas now, I bought every inch of the motherhood narrative as a young woman. Indeed, it was all I prayed about and dreamed of for a very long time.

Yet, as the years wore on and I didn't get pregnant and had no children to show for the love E and I shared, my shame began to grow legs. Running amok throughout my mind, body, and spirit, I wore the shame of being a childless and infertile woman like a person wears an animal skin to stay warm in the wintertime.

Truth be told, it didn't bother me that E married Penninah. He was doing what he was supposed to do as a Hebrew man. I understood his duty, and I grieved that I could not fulfill mine.

The way our story has been told—Penninah and me—you'd think we were enemies. Instead, we were more like distant relatives. We interacted with many of the same people. We lived in the same encampment. I joined the other women in the birthing tent when she gave birth, as was the custom for women who'd started bleeding each month. But we didn't talk much. I averted her eyes. Our interactions were surface-level and sparse.

Do you need water from the well?

Here, take some bread for dinner.

Yes, I'll be at Auntie's celebration next month.

We never spoke of Elkanah, and we never spoke of their child. It was best for me, or so I thought, to pretend he didn't exist.

* * *

Which is why, when Penninah approached me as I slopped on the ground that fateful, emotionally laden, horrible day, initially I was shocked. We'd never uttered more than a few words to each other, much less spoken about God, the absurd expectations placed upon women, and shame.

My defenses wanted to scream at her. "Who do you think you are? You don't know me!"

My surrendering, prayerful spirit, instead, led me to listen, to receive.

After she left, I laid on the ground for a long time. And though she said some beautiful things, what I kept replaying in my mind was the idea (the truth, perhaps?) that God is not a punitive asshole. That maybe God really was with me in kindness and love, pregnant, not pregnant, perfect, imperfect. That perhaps I was pretending God was in control when, really, I was acting and living like I was.

* * *

"I'm going to Shiloh," I declared one morning over breakfast.

E raised his eyebrows and said, "Oh? Are you now?"

"I am," I stated.

"Okay, dear," he said lovingly. "I'll help you pack."

E learned a long time ago that it was best to leave me be when I'd made up my mind about something. In this way, he was a wise man.

Shiloh was where the Ark of the Covenant lived, and at that sacred place, I knew I could pour out my deepest concerns before God. Ever since I was young, I needed something to see and touch when I prayed. A simple altar set with a candle and spices. A cloth I could hold close to me in bed. The tangible nature of such things helped me believe God could be that close to me and that real, too.

So, the Ark, with its gold, acacia wood, and ornate cherubim called to me. At its Mercy Seat I would find God, and God would find me, and, perhaps, this would help me have a son? Feel less shame? Lay down even half of what I'd been carrying all these years?

* * *

Approaching the Ark was like approaching God. Or, at least, what I imagined approaching God would be like. It was like it was lit from within and hovering in space without need for fixture or frame. The Ark beckoned me nearer and nearer.

"Holy of Holy," I whispered, "I am here by your grace."

Kneeling, I lifted my hands upward and began to cry. My tears were my most honest prayer. I had no more questions to ask or promises to make. I simply had the water and salt of my body to pour out like incense before the Holy.

Almost trancelike, I didn't hear the priest, Eli, approaching me. I jumped when I felt his hand on my shoulder.

"Excuse me, ma'am," he stuttered, "but I must ask, as the priest of this temple, are you drunk?"

Leave it to a man to think that a woman pouring out her deepest, most fervent desires before God is drunk.

Taking a deep breath, quickly wiping the tears from my face, I looked Eli in the eyes and said, "I'm not drunk. I'm sad. The only thing I've poured out today is my soul before the Lord."

"All is well then," Eli said, attempting to laugh off his gaffe. "The Lord will grant your petition."

He said it with such confidence and flippancy, as if he knew what I'd been praying. As if he himself were God.

Deep down, somewhere dark and hidden, though, I hoped that he'd be right.

* * *

On the journey home, I took ashes from cedar and mesquite and scattered them along the pilgrim's path. An ancient ritual of release, every few steps I would rub my hands in the ashes until they were darker than a storm cloud. Then, I would spit into my hands, rub them together, and then thrust them outward away from my heart, singing:

Every desire I give to God.

Every hope I release into the unknown.

Every prayer I entrust to Mystery.

I let go. I let go. I let go.

I hadn't given up on the dream of having a son, but I had loosened my grip on it just enough so that I could find a way to live even if I never became a mother. Walking mile after mile, praying with my feet along the pilgrim's path, I began to understand that surrender was not defeat but victory, that allowing life to be as it was—not as I longed for it to be—was not giving up. Rather, it was peace, flowing like a river to the depths of my soul.

All things, of course, Penninah shared with me in a quiet, gentle voice as I laid, unmoving and prostrate, on the ground that day. Letting go, after all, is only possible when you trust yourself (and the God you believe in) enough to know that you don't let go into a void of nothingness. Rather, you let go into a vastness of love. When I began to learn this vast, forever love, I began to loosen my grip. I began to be a little more free.

* * *

When I learned I was pregnant, I did not cry. Instead, I laughed. Joy billowed up and out of me. I danced and laughed, laughed and danced the night away.

I was pregnant with Samuel, his name meaning, "God has heard my cry," and yet what God heard that night were not my cries but my giggles and howls under the bright, full moon. Though Penninah was nowhere to be seen, I like to think she was dancing and howling along with me, celebrating from afar what I'd wanted for so long.

Did God hear me every day, every week, every month, every year that I begged for a son? She must have. But it wasn't God who got me pregnant (contrary to what my mama told me when I was ten). That was between E and me. But God *was* with me every time I bled, every time I traveled, every time I sang, every time I questioned, every time I cried. As Penninah proclaimed, God is the God of presence, and it was and still is Her presence that carries me through.

* * *

As soon as Samuel was born, a child with wild hair and dark eyes, I knew we'd dedicate him to the Nazirite priesthood. I had said as much on my way back from Shiloh—*Every desire I give to God. Every hope I release into the unknown. Every prayer I entrust to Mystery. I let go. I let go. I let go.*

From the outside looking in, what irony. I had waited all these years to have a baby and now that I had one, I was choosing to give him away.

Sometimes mothers choose seemingly odd things for the sake of our children and our God. Until you've walked in our sandals or lived in our bodies, it's best not to judge us. Instead, what if you came alongside us like God? What if you listened to us, learned from us, and loved with us?

* * *

Though E and I dedicated Samuel to the priesthood, I was never too far away from Shiloh or from Samuel. I'd been a pilgrim for far too long to let go of the spiritual practice now. Every few months, I would pack my bags, journey to the Holy of Holies, and continue to pray and to sing, foreshadowing the prayers and songs of innumerable other women whose songs and voices would carry an entire people on the notes of their melodies.

Once there, Samuel and I would lock eyes from a distance. We would smile and offer a slight lift of the chin, our way of saying, "I see you. I know you." We spoke a thousand words without ever saying a thing.

* * *

"Perhaps only prophets can birth other prophets," I say to Penninah as we sit, side by side, under a mesquite tree. "Perhaps Samuel is only 'heard by God' because I was heard by Her first," I continue.

Penninah nods her head, listening.

We are friends now, Penninah and me. An unlikely friendship, certainly, but nevertheless a holy one. We still don't say a whole lot to each other, preferring each other's quiet company to waxing eloquently about our lives.

Most of the time we sing together. We praise God, not for getting us pregnant, but for never leaving our sides. We sing because it's the most natural response to joy we can offer.

* * *

I like to think that I would've sung the song that became known as mine whether I had Samuel or not. Who's to ever really know?

What I *do* know is that my song is really *our* song—Penninah, me, and all who long for freedom in a world that keeps us tied to systems we struggle to transform. It is a song I cannot sing, *will not* sing without the untold women who sang it before me. It is a song that is sung by countless women after me. It is a song of joy. It is a song of liberation. It is a song of longing, love, and letting go.

I can't promise that singing will heal every wound or repair every problem, but I can testify to its healing powers in my own life as a woman, mother, prophet, and friend.

Will you sing with Penninah and me? Will you sing with God? Will you sing with yourself? Will you sing with the women? Singing, the language of the divine feminine, just might birth in us something in addition to children. Singing just might birth in us that which sets us (and others) free.

It was never my fault, and it's not yours either. Whatever it is that you think you've done wrong or poorly, whatever it is you think is unforgiveable in you, the Holy of Holies is not a punitive asshole doling out punishments like a judge on high. No, the Holy of Holies is the one whispering within you, "You are love. You are loved." Amen.

My heart rejoices in Love;

I smile at the voices both within me and outside of me

that taunt and ridicule, attack and accuse,

for they need compassion, too.

No one is holy like You;

No one is loving like You;

No one holds us steady like You.

We pray that we will be slow to speak,

Fast to listen. For only You are truly wise.

With You, everything turns.

The hungry hunger no more.
The childless give birth
again and again and again.
The poor no longer want.
The marginalized come to the center.
From the ashes, we rise and inherit
the goodness of community, the promise
that patriarchy has no place in the
kin-dom of God.
For this is like heaven to us.
For this is like freedom in us.

You guard the feet of women
and those who love and support us.
You silence the arrogant ones
and remind us, yet again,
that true strength comes
from within.
Though the world can break us
into thousands upon thousands of pieces,
though we fracture and fragment
ourselves till we are close to death,
You raise us up as prophets,
singing your mercies,
bestowing your grace,
exalting the praises of You and Yours faithfully, forever.

LITURGY FOR EVENING PRAYER

Opening Proclamation

May everything that has breath praise Elohim!

May even the rocks cry out in song as we praise the goodness of our God!

Evening Prayer

As the sun fades, shedding golden light on this day,

we pray that You, O God, might sing in us and through us,

as we convey in song what we have a hard time speaking aloud.

Humbling heartbreak. Overwhelming joy. Honest frustration. Wonder and worry.

May the vibrations of our voices loosen in us what needs loosening.

May the notes of the melody hold us when we need holding.

May we make a joyful, honest noise to you and with you, O God, we pray. **Amen.**

Psalm 100 (inspired by the Common English Bible translation)

Shout out loud! Let your longings be heard throughout the land!

God created us to sing. We belong to God's chorus of love.

Use your voice! Sing your truth to God and others!

God created us to sing. We belong to God's chorus of love.

Stand in gratitude with your hands open to the sky! Tread lightly upon the earth that is God's body! Hum melodies of blessing everywhere you go.

God created us to sing. We belong to God's chorus of Love.

Sing the song of God's goodness and love. Sing the song of God's justice and mercy. Sing the song of God's healing and hope.

God created us to sing. We belong to God's chorus of Love.

Scripture Reading: 1 Samuel 2

The Song of Hannah.

Thanks be to God.

A moment of quiet for prayer and reflection.

Song of Praise

In the Beginning

Claire K. McKeever-Burgett

Contemporary Connection

Take a few moments to listen to and watch "Letting Go" *by Angie McMahon, and "Requiem" by Allison Russell.*[21] *Imagine Hannah singing these songs as she walks home from Shiloh. Imagine yourself singing them as a prayer of blessing and letting go. Invite these songs into your prayerful, worshipful, songful life.*

[21] McKeever-Burgett, Claire, *Music for Contemporary Connections,* https://www.clairemckeeverburgett.com/*music, accessed July 10, 2025.*

The Prayer of the Women

Holy Mother of sand and sea,
to You all honor and praise.
When we cry out, You hear us.
When we ask for help, You help us.
When we long to be loved, You love us.
May mercy be offered to everyone.
May power and dominion over others cease.
May greed and violence end.
May love live forever.
Birth us into a new world.
Help us make this one beautiful.
Stir us up. Settle us down.
Burn. Simmer. Refine.
When all else shakes, hold us steady.
When everyone else wants to blame,
remind us that in You there is only Love.
Our praise and our prayers are Yours, forever. Amen.
Blessing and Sending Forth
Loosen our grip, Mother God,
that we might cling only to You. **Amen.**

REFLECTION QUESTIONS

The following questions are meant to deepen and expand, invite and beckon thoughtful, compassionate, and curious responses to the story and liturgy of Hannah. Whether considering these questions on your own or in a group setting, create space for journaling, collaging, or painting in response. If engaging in group discussion, choose one or two questions at most to hold at the center of your sacred circle.

1. What resonates with you about Hannah's story? What feels redemptive? What feels challenging?

2. When singing along with Hannah, Mother God, and the women, what sensations do you notice in your body?
3. What song do you want to sing to yourself and to God?
4. Think of a time in your life when you dedicated something or someone to God. What did that feel like and look like for you?
5. On what could you loosen your grip right now, and how might loosening your grip help ease your mind, body, and spirit?

PUBLIC WITNESS

Because what good are our prayers on Sunday if they make no meaning in our lives on Monday?

Part of our calling as people who claim to follow a God of love, justice, and mercy is to connect what we pray, sing, and hear on Sundays (or the day we set aside to worship God) to the whole of our lives. How does what we pray one day affect where we spend our time and financial resources on another day? How does praying for, about, and with women affect how we vote and whom we serve? God's loving call in Deuteronomy 6:5, "You shall love the Lord our God with all your heart, all your soul, and all your strength," commands us to integrate our faith into every aspect of our lives, which includes bearing witness to the good, necessary, and powerful work of justice-seeking, beauty-creating, love-making women in the world today.

Hannah likely suffered from a perinatal mental health issue, common to many birthing people, particularly those who suffer infertility. Hannah, like all birthing people, deserved access to the support she needed as she navigated the psychological, spiritual, and emotional toll of infertility in a world dominated by a system that rendered her invaluable if she couldn't produce children.

The **Perinatal Mental Health Alliance for People of Color (PMHA-POC)** is bridging the gap in perinatal mental health support services for birthing persons, providers, and communities of color. A fully funded program within Postpartum Support International, PMHA-POC increases the capacity of perinatal professionals to support individuals, families, and communities of color around perinatal mood and anxiety disorders.

Learn more about this organization. Continue to support groups in your own communities that promote awareness, advocacy, and support for those experiencing perinatal mental health issues. Connect. Learn. Give. Grow.[22]

[22] McKeever-Burgett, Claire, *Public Witness Woman-Led Nonprofits, https://www.clairemckeeverburgett.com/public-witness, accessed July 10, 2025.*

Part Three

Wise women know that the deepest wisdom they will ever find is the wisdom that lives within. Wise women in the Hebrew Bible may have represented a civic leadership role during the period of the judges and early monarchy. Women called "wise" were often known for their wise judgment, clear communication skills, and ability to negotiate difficult situations. Wisdom itself is personified as a woman in the book of Proverbs, and I have taken the liberty to give these personifications names and stories as if they were actual wise women who lived among the people. Of utmost importance here, though, is that women have been sought out for their wisdom since the beginning of time.

Chapter Nine

Adah

Beauty Maker | Proverbs 31:10–31

Adah (name): of Hebrew origin meaning "adornment" or "beautiful"

* * *

A capable wife who can find?
She is far more precious than jewels.
The heart of her husband trusts in her,
and he will have no lack of gain.
She does him good, and not harm,
all the days of her life.
She seeks wool and flax,
and works with willing hands.
She is like the ships of the merchant,
she brings her food from far away.
She rises while it is still night
and provides food for her household
and tasks for her servant-girls.
She considers a field and buys it;
with the fruit of her hands she plants a vineyard.
She girds herself with strength,
and makes her arms strong.
She perceives that her merchandise is profitable.
Her lamp does not go out at night.
She puts her hands to the distaff,
and her hands hold the spindle.
She opens her hand to the poor,
and reaches out her hands to the needy.
She is not afraid for her household when it snows,
for all her household are clothed in crimson.

She makes herself coverings;
her clothing is fine linen and purple.
Her husband is known in the city gates,
taking his seat among the elders of the land.
She makes linen garments and sells them;
she supplies the merchant with sashes.
Strength and dignity are her clothing,
and she laughs at the time to come.
She opens her mouth with wisdom,
and the teaching of kindness is on her tongue.
She looks well to the ways of her household,
and does not eat the bread of idleness.
Her children rise up and call her happy;
her husband too, and he praises her:
'Many women have done excellently,
but you surpass them all.'
Charm is deceitful, and beauty is vain,
but a woman who fears the LORD *is to be praised.*
Give her a share in the fruit of her hands,
and let her works praise her in the city gates.

—Proverbs 31:10–31

* * *

ADAH'S STORY

I am Adah, the one adorned. A woman of the same name was married to Esau. Another woman of the same name gave birth to Jabal and Jubal. Contrary to popular belief, to be adorned had very little to do with outward appearance and much more to do with the adornment of inner gifts—gifts only seen through how one lives: with integrity, honesty, forthrightness, and love.

You're only as beautiful as you treat the ugliest person in the room, my grandmother used to say.

Sure, the men who got to name us cared about what we looked like. But we knew our lives had much more to offer than outward appearance, production, and performance. In fact, it was knowing that our worth depended on much more than external appearance that kept us alive.

More than wives and mothers, we Adahs were creators of strategies that helped whole nations exist and grow. We listened carefully. We devised plans. We inscribed those plans on stones. We were preservers of culture and community.

We told stories. We spun tales. We sang songs. We wove together words like scraps of fabric, creating liturgies of praise to the God who provided, forgave, and loved.

We made fires and cooked food. We planted it, grew it, and harvested it. We fed the world from our bodies, our hands, our minds, our work.

With us, the world was made.

* * *

When I was a young girl, my grandmother looked me in the eyes and said, "When I die, do not visit my grave with incense and flowers. Honor me by the way you live."

She said this to me one muggy afternoon while the men of our family packed their bags, readying themselves for the graveyard where they would bow with gifts at the graves of their mothers and grandmothers. She refused to go with them.

"Nope. Not doing it," she mumbled as she kneaded the bread, preparing it for baking. "They won't make a mockery of me and my kind. I'll demand honor now, not later. And if they won't give it, fine. I'd rather not have it at all than to have it only once I'm gone."

As a girl, I was in awe of her. As a grown woman, I am indebted to her.

Though I didn't know it at the time, I understand now that this was her act of resistance to a system set up to use and discard women while they were alive only to revere them when they were dead. That was too little, too late.

It's not that she had no mercy; it's that she knew she wasn't God, and she knew she didn't want to be. She left the mercy up to the

Merciful One. She stood on her own sacred ground, demanding, in her own small yet powerful way, accountability from a system that would likely never give it. Undeterred, she died trying, and I love her for it.

***

I often think of my grandmother's admonishment. Locked jaw. Big eyes. Furrowed brow. What wouldn't I give to have her with me now for one more bread-kneading session? To hear her mumble, to bask in her determination.

I haven't always lived what society would call a "perfect life." I've been drunk on wine. I've been with a lot of men *and* women. I've traveled both near and far. I've waited to have children. I've said *no* when they wanted me to say *yes*.

Throughout the years, as messages from my religious culture have ridiculed, side-eyed, and judged me, I've wondered, "Am I honoring my grandmother with my life? Am I letting her down? Am I doing what she instructed me to do?"

Even the best of us is prone to wander. Even the wisest among us let doubt creep in.

But as my grandmother taught me to do, instead of running away from the doubt or ignoring the wandering spirit, I've stayed with them. I've taken them into my calloused hands and marveled at their persistence.

What is it you want to teach me? I've asked them. *What is it you want me to know?*

Slowly, surely, I've heard the answers—answers that were less about moral purity and more about seeking justice, loving mercy, and walking humbly. Answers less about who I've slept with and more about coming home to myself. Answers less about where I've been and more about where I currently am. Answers less about what is right and more about what is honest, trustworthy, true.

Honoring my grandmother with my life turns out to have everything to do with actually living it and learning from it.

***

The longer I live, the more I visit the water's edge, a place where I can be still and listen. A place where I can dip my hand into the cool water, bring it to my face, blessing every inch of me.

Here, where the water flows, I sing a song for my grandmother, myself, and all the women who've made me who I am. Because, after all, we exist because of one another. We make the way together.

Sometimes I hear my grandmother singing with me. Sometimes I see her splashing in the water. Other times, she's difficult to conjure, harder to find. Still, the water, snaking its way through the earth, reminds me that the wet pool in which I bathe is the same river in which she bathed, too.

* * *

"When I die," I say to my granddaughter, "Sing."

"What do I sing?" she asks.

"A song about women's honesty and strength. A song about how they wouldn't have any of it without us," I reply.

She nods her head, closes her eyes, and reaches for my wrinkled, blue-veined hands. She opens her mouth and begins to sing what I've been singing to her since she was born—*Women of Integrity, Everywhere.*

As the melody fills the space between us, the birds join the song with their harmonies, the trees with their percussion, the river with its soft hum. All of creation sings with us. All of creation knows that we are women of integrity, that our song is worth singing, and that we, like creation itself, are everywhere.

Listen closely the next time you walk in the woods or rest by a river or swim in the ocean. If you can become quiet enough, you will hear wisdom's song singing, and you, like each of us, will know it's always been the women of integrity who help make the world anew.

* * *

Women of Integrity, Everywhere, a rendering of Proverbs 31:10–31

Who can find a woman of integrity?
I can. I am surrounded by them.

Honest and trustworthy women are everywhere.
Without them, I would not be. Without them, no one would be.
Listen to women speak. Place confidence in our leadership.
Married or unmarried, our relationship status does not determine our worth.
Our lives center the poor and those traditionally pushed to the margins.
Our hearts remain wide open to love.

We strategize and craft; we build and play; we birth and deliver.
We welcome and listen; we cure and communicate; we find our voices, and we use them.
We bring forth life and fight like hell to make that life worth living.
We stand on sacred ground. We listen to the Holy.
We circle around flames to process, listen, and dance.
We are the flame itself.
We laugh. We sing. We tell the truth.
Wisdom, our birthright. Power to choose, our dignity.
Creativity, our essence. Rest, our promise.

We know we are beautiful, not because of how we look, but because of who we are—women, not of men, but in contrast to them. Different, not to procreate but to stand our sacred ground as the creators, leaders, wisdom-bearers that we are.

For all our hands have made,
For all our hands continue to make,
All praise, all glory, all honor be unto women
and to the God who created us holy, sacred, divine, and good.
Amen.

LITURGY FOR MIDDAY PRAYER

OPENING

If you are gathered with others, position yourselves in a circle. Place a lit candle in the center. If you are alone, light a candle as a sign of connection to Mother God and to the circle of women who join you, even here, even now, as you pray.

Call to Prayer

God who created us holy, sacred, divine, good,

We pause to breathe in Your presence here and now.

Pause for deep breathing in through the mouth, out through the nose.

Prayer at Midday

Holy Mother God, we've lived at least three lifetimes since we woke up this morning.

We've fed mouths and told stories and hugged necks and led meetings and balanced budgets and eased anxiety. To say we need to rest in You is an understatement. Here we are, breathing in Your presence, trusting that You, too, know what it's like to need to rest. Be with us now. Rest with us now, we pray. Amen.

Psalm 119:105–112 (inspired by the Common English Bible)

Your presence, O God, is a light for our path, a guide for our way.

We fully mean it when we say that we love you, we trust you, we know you and your wisdom within us.

We've been going too fast for too long. We're out of breath, tired, and afraid. God, help us live again according to your promise of abundance and love.

Teach us what it means to listen to our grandmothers. Accept our gifts of praise to our ancestors and to You who always and ever guided them.

Though our lives are threatened by the rules of patriarchy, help us remember Your Way of Love.

Though we are taught as women that we must act and look and be a certain way or else we are wrong, help us remember that is a bald-faced lie.

Your Love liberates us to live in our bodies, minds, and spirits as You created us. Every shape, size, color, and expression are beautiful to You. Being fully ourselves is joy and justice.

Because Your presence frees us from lies that would keep us from loving ourselves and the world You love, we will follow Your way, O God, and keep Your Love in our hearts forever. **Amen.**

Women of Integrity, Everywhere, a rendering of Proverbs 31:10–31

Who can find a woman of integrity?
I can. I am surrounded by them.
Honest and trustworthy women are everywhere.
Without them, I would not be. Without them, no one would be.
Listen to women speak. Place confidence in our leadership.
Married or unmarried, our relationship status does not determine our worth.
Our lives center the poor and those traditionally pushed to the margins.
Our hearts remain wide open to love.
We strategize and craft; we build and play; we birth and deliver.
We welcome and listen; we cure and communicate; we find our voices, and we use them.
We bring forth life and fight like hell to make that life worth living.
We stand on sacred ground. We listen to the Holy.
We circle around flames to process, hear, and dance.
We are the flame itself.
We laugh. We sing. We tell the truth.
Wisdom, our birthright. Power to choose, our dignity.
Creativity, our essence. Rest, our promise.
We know we are beautiful, not because of how we look, but because of who we are—women, not of men, but in contrast to them. Different, not to procreate but to stand our sacred ground as the creators, leaders, wisdom-bearers that we are.
For all our hands have made,
For all our hands continue to make,
All praise. All glory. All honor be unto women
and to the God who created us holy, sacred, divine, good.
Amen.

Hold a moment of quiet for prayer and reflection.

Song of Praise

In the Beginning

Claire K. McKeever-Burgett

Contemporary Connection

Take a few moments to listen and watch "Hymn for a Woman" by That Woman a.k.a. Josephine Vander West.[23] *Imagine Adah singing this song with her grandmother, mother, daughters, and granddaughters. Imagine yourself singing it as a song to yourself and to the woman of integrity you are and are becoming. Invite this song into your prayerful, worshipful, songful life.*

The Prayer of the Women

Holy Mother of sand and sea,

to You all honor and praise.

When we cry out, You hear us.

When we ask for help, You help us.

When we long to be loved, You love us.

May mercy be offered to everyone.

May power and dominion over others cease.

May greed and violence end.

---

[23] McKeever-Burgett, Claire, *Music for Contemporary Connections,* https://www.clairemckeeverburgett.com/*music, accessed July 10, 2025.*

May love live forever.

Birth us into a new world.

Help us make this one beautiful.

Stir us up. Settle us down.

Burn. Simmer. Refine.

When all else shakes, hold us steady.

When everyone else wants to blame,

remind us that in You there is only Love.

Our praise and our prayers are Yours, forever. Amen.

Closing Blessing

May we see and honor the integrity of all. May we see and know the beauty of all. May we see and celebrate the complexity and depth of all. For the glory of You, Mother God, who created us in Your image and called us good, very, very good. Amen.

REFLECTION QUESTIONS

The following questions are meant to deepen and expand, invite and beckon thoughtful, compassionate, and curious responses to the story and liturgy of Adah. Whether considering these questions on your own or in a group setting, create space for journaling, collaging, or painting in response. If engaging in group discussion, choose one or two questions, at most, to hold at the center of your sacred circle.

1. What resonates with you about Adah's story and the interpretation of Proverbs 31:10–31? What feels redemptive? What feels challenging?
2. When reading and praying with Adah, Mother God, and the women, what sensations do you notice in your body?
3. What narratives about women and societal expectations of how they're supposed to be do you need to reconsider or rewrite considering Adah's story?
4. How do you want to be honored after you die?

PUBLIC WITNESS

Because what good are our prayers on Sunday if they make no meaning in our lives on Monday?

Part of our calling as people who claim to follow a God of love, justice, and mercy is to connect what we pray, sing, and hear on Sundays (or the day we set aside to worship God) to the whole of our lives. How does what we pray one day affect where we spend our time and financial resources on another day? How does praying for, about, and with women affect how we vote and who we serve? God's loving call in Deuteronomy 6:5, "You shall love the Lord your God with all your heart, all your soul, and all your strength," commands us to integrate our faith into every aspect of our lives, which includes bearing witness to the good, necessary, and powerful work of justice-seeking, beauty-creating, love-making women in the world today.

Adah offers us a vision of a woman who's doing the work of integration—taking what she knows in her head down into the deepest parts of her heart and soul. Multidimensional and free, Adah's story leads me to the modern-day work of **Womankind Worldwide: A Feminist Ecosystem for Change**, which seeks to create a world in which women, girls, and people of all genders enjoy equal rights and freedoms and live with joy, choice, and dignity. Adah's story also led me to **Beautiful Trouble,** which equips social movements with an ever-growing suite of strategic tools and training to help grassroots movements be more creative, effective, and irresistible.

Learn more about these organizations. Continue to support organizations in your own communities that support women's mind, body, and spirit integration, dignity, and freedom. Connect. Learn. Give. Grow.[24]

---

[24] McKeever-Burgett, Claire, *Public Witness Woman-Led Nonprofits, https://www.clairemckeeverburgett.com/public-witness, accessed July 10, 2025.*

Chapter Ten

Eliora

Truthteller and Lightbearer | 1 Samuel 28:3–25

Eliora (name): of Hebrew origin meaning "God is my light"

* * *

Now Samuel had died, and all Israel had mourned for him and buried him in Ramah, his own city. Saul had expelled the mediums and the wizards from the land. The Philistines assembled and came and encamped at Shunem. Saul gathered all Israel, and they encamped at Gilboa. When Saul saw the army of the Philistines, he was afraid, and his heart trembled greatly. When Saul inquired of the Lord, the Lord did not answer him, not by dreams or by Urim or by prophets. Then Saul said to his servants, "Seek out for me a woman who is a medium, so that I may go to her and inquire of her." His servants said to him, "There is a medium at Endor."

So Saul disguised himself and put on other clothes and went there, he and two men with him. They came to the woman by night. And he said, "Consult a spirit for me, and bring up for me the one whom I name to you." The woman said to him, "Surely you know what Saul has done, how he has cut off the mediums and the wizards from the land. Why then are you laying a snare for my life to bring about my death?" But Saul swore to her by the Lord, "As the Lord lives, no punishment shall come upon you for this thing." Then the woman said, "Whom shall I bring up for you?" He answered, "Bring up Samuel for me." When the woman saw Samuel, she cried out with a loud voice, and the woman said to Saul, "Why have you deceived me? You are Saul!" The king said to her, "Have no fear; what do you see?" The woman said to Saul, "I see a divine being coming up out of the ground." He said to her, "What is his appearance?" She said, "An old man is coming up; he is wrapped in a robe." So Saul knew that it was Samuel, and he bowed with his face to the ground and did obeisance.

Then Samuel said to Saul, "Why have you disturbed me by bringing me up?" Saul answered, "I am in great distress, for the Philistines are warring against me, and God has turned away from me and answers me no more, either by prophets or by dreams, so I have summoned you to tell me what I should do." Samuel said, "Why then do you ask me, since the Lord has turned from you and become your enemy? The Lord has done to you just as he spoke by me, for the Lord has torn the kingdom out of your hand and given it to your neighbor, David. Because you did not obey the voice of the Lord and did not carry out his fierce wrath against Amalek, therefore the Lord has done this thing to you today. Moreover, the Lord will give Israel along with you into the hands of the Philistines, and tomorrow you and your sons shall be with me; the Lord will also give the army of Israel into the hands of the Philistines."

Immediately Saul fell full length on the ground filled with fear because of the words of Samuel, and there was no strength in him, for he had eaten nothing all day and all night. The woman came to Saul, and when she saw that he was terrified, she said to him, "Your servant has listened to you; I have taken my life in my hand and have listened to what you have said to me. Now, therefore, you also listen to your servant; let me set a morsel of bread before you. Eat, that you may have strength when you go on your way." He refused and said, "I will not eat." But his servants, together with the woman, urged him, and he listened to their words. So he got up from the ground and sat on the bed. Now the woman had a fatted calf in the house. She quickly slaughtered it, and she took flour, kneaded it, and baked unleavened cakes. She put them before Saul and his servants, and they ate. Then they rose and went away that night.

—1 Samuel 28:3–25

* * *

ELIORA'S STORY

I am only four years old when I witness the first spell being cast. Awakened by whispers and light, I walk toward the sounds and the visions, desperate to know more.

From the small entranceway, I see my mother and grandmother, a few of their friends, and one of my aunts. They encircle a fire, and they dance in rhythm with one another and with the fire itself.

Grandmother begins to chant something I cannot understand. Mother waves her arms and throws something into the flames. The others sway and breathe, moved by something other than themselves.

Before they can see me, I scamper back to bed, though I lie awake the rest of the night, amazed and perplexed by what I witnessed.

A few days later, Mother comes to me.

"Do you want to know what we were doing the other night, baby girl?" she asks as she moves a strand of my hair behind my ear.

"How did you know I was there?" my little voice shakes, afraid I will be in trouble.

"I saw your shadow," she says. "It's okay. We all learn at some point."

"What, Mama? What do we learn?"

"That we are witches," she answers.

"What does that mean?" I ask her, confused and a little afraid.

"As you grow, you will learn," she says. "I will be here to teach you. We witches cast spells and dream dreams and see what others won't."

Though I do not know what she means, I trust her completely. Crawling into her lap, laying my head on her heart, I close my eyes and breathe. She smells of campfire and dirt, madness and mystery, and as I drift off to sleep, I remember thinking that she and all she is will forever be my home.

* * *

The night Mother died, we gathered around her bed. With oils and herbs, songs and prayers, we accompanied her to death. As I had done when I was four, I laid my head on her chest. I could still hear the faint beating of her heart, though it slowed with every labored breath she took.

"I love you," I whispered. "I will carry on our work."

Though she could no longer speak, and it was questionable whether she could hear much, if anything, her hand grazed my hair. I felt as if she heard me, and that she knew that I would proudly inhabit my role as a witch, carrying on the women's work of our family, carrying on what wisdom I could discern and what madness I could make clear.

She took her last breath when the last star faded from the predawn sky. I cried. The women surrounded me with their presence and love.

* * *

For many years, we witches lived as part of society, our role as diviners of God's truth understood as essential in the life of the community. However, after Samuel died, Saul issued a decree: ALL WITCHCRAFT & SORCERY BANNED! ANY WHO ARE FOUND PRACTICING AS A MEDIUM OR A WITCH WILL BE PUNISHED BY DEATH!

I was old when the decree was made, so I kept to myself in the cave in which my family had lived for many years. Content communicating with the spirits on my own time, in my own ways, without any witnesses, I trusted I would be left alone in the womb-like darkness where things didn't need to be crystal clear because Love surrounded me, and that always felt enough.

Contrary to popular thought, the darkness illuminated truth rather than hid it. Perhaps Saul knew this deep down, though he'd never admit it. Why else would he show up at my doorstep in the dead of night?

There were three men at the entrance to the cave, imploring me to consult a spirit. I didn't know that it was Saul, though I would soon discover his identity.

Still, I told them the truth. "Conjuring spirits is banned by the king. I'm not willing to die for you."

One of them was persistent and, swearing by God, said, "I assure you, in Hashem's presence, you will not be harmed. I need you to see what I can't see!"

"Oh, sir. That's where you have it wrong. It's not that I see what you can't; it's that I see what you won't."

Stammering, the persistent one asked, "Well, what won't I see? Tell me! Tell me!"

He was desperate and afraid. I was quiet and confident. Channeling my mother and my grandmother, I resigned myself to help him, despite the king's decree. That's the thing with witches: we cannot help but be who we are.

* * *

I invited them in to sit by the glowing ashes. My nighttime fire was almost burned out. I walked in a circle around the ashes, using my hands to dance with the rising smoke.

"Breathe it in," I said. "Soften your hearts. Open your minds. The dead only visit when we prepare ourselves for their presence."

"Who do you wish to see?" I asked, breathing in the flame.

"The priest, prophet, and judge, Samuel," he replied.

By speaking Samuel's name, I immediately knew who was sitting in front of me. Samuel, the last judge of Israel, was the King's closest advisor before he died. The way Saul said Samuel's name revealed he knew him well and suggested deep, deep love.

"Why have you lied to me, King Saul?" I whispered.

"You need not fear. I will not retaliate," he said in response. "What do you see?"

"You didn't answer me," I whispered again. "Why have you lied to me?"

Saul had nothing to say. He refused to admit that he was afraid. He was terrified of confessing that he, as a powerful king, could not discern the next way forward without the help of a witch.

I hesitated, letting the smoke rise, letting the truth simmer. Silence was our friend.

Finally, I broke the silence and said, "You lie to your people. You malign my craft, you disrespect ancient wisdom. Yet, here you are, begging for a miracle. I should throw you out of my cave now."

Saul continued to beg. "What do you see? Please tell me."

Stopping in my tracks, facing the smoldering fire, I reached for the earth. With dirt under my nails, I brought my hands to my face, covering it with mud.

Then, I began to hum and sway. "Whoever needs to speak, speak. You are welcome here," I chanted.

Again, Saul, with his whiny desperation, "What do you see? Who is it?"

"A divine being," I replied.

"What does it look like?" Saul inquired.

"I see an old man, wrapped in a robe."

Hearing this description, Saul bowed to the ground. We both knew Samuel was with us.

Then, speaking through me, Samuel asked Saul, "Why have you disturbed me?"

"Because," Saul cried, "I'm in great distress. The Philistines are coming for me. God no longer answers me through prophets or in dreams. So here I am with a witch, begging you to tell me what I should do."

"Her name is Eliora," Samuel said through me.

Saul's face twitched and contorted. He was not one to show fear. He was not one to be corrected.

"If God has turned from you," Samuel asked through me, "Why do you think I will help? God is doing what God said God would do: the kingdom is torn out of your hands because you did not obey the Holy One. Israel will be delivered to the Philistines, and, tomorrow, your sons will be with me."

Channeling Samuel's voice through my own, I levitated off the ground, floating above Saul as he wept. Saul laid prostrate on the floor of the cave, unable to move.

When Samuel left us, I returned to the earth, this time taking a seat next to Saul.

Apparently neither Saul nor his companions had eaten all day, and so I fed them.

Still, we cannot live on bread alone but by every word that comes from God.[25] And Samuel's words speaking through me to Saul were the words of God—forceful, decisive, and true.

That night, I offered a word, a meal, and a vision.

Saul and his friends left once they gained the energy to do so, and what Samuel proclaimed would happen, did indeed happen.

The Israelite army was defeated; Saul's sons died; and Saul himself was wounded and then committed suicide by falling on his sword.

I heard all of this after the fact. Word traveled slowly in those days. But when I heard it, I wasn't surprised. Still, I took stones, struck them together, and made a fire.

"God who is my light," I sang, "Receive Saul into your fold. Receive all who long to know the truth into your fold. God who is my light, be light to others."

It was my witchy way of honoring Saul and others who, despite their shortcomings and ignorance, still deserved to be honored and released into to the hands and light of God. It's what we all receive in the end, regardless of who we are.

* * *

My name is Eliora, meaning my God is my light, which, is ironic given that I did most of my work in the dark of night. However, God's light is not only a bright, blinding beam. It is also a soft, present glow that allows one to see by the moon and the stars, guided more by what

---

[25] Deuteronomy 8:3.

is hidden than by what is seen. Those of us who see by the light of God trust the path that is only made clear by walking it.

Witches, sorcerers, and mediums may be closest to God in the sense that our connection to the natural world, to all created beings, to seeing things as they are, not as we want them to be, is part of what enables us to know what we know, see what we see, and move what we move. It's part of what enables us to be diviners of the truth.

I wish all women knew of their inherent witchiness, their ability to look within and know the power that pulses through their veins. Born to fly, witchy women are only scary if you fear what is true.

Hence, being a witch has very little to do with sorcery and magic and much more to do with claiming the power within. It has very little to do with potions and dreams and much more to do with connecting to a community of truth-tellers.

A friend of mine said of us witches, "All we do is hold up a mirror so people can see things clearly."[26]

* * *

Since my encounter with Saul and Samuel, I've wondered what to make of it. I've pondered what is so threatening about my work as a witch, why people have killed me and my kind for years, why Saul banned us from doing our work. Why, after my power and my presence spoke truth and set a table, I carried the blame for Saul's death.[27]

As if witchcraft were meant to destroy! As if witchcraft wields the power only Elohim possesses!

The night Saul visited me, and Samuel spoke through me, there were many spirits present. God, not a singular being, was a chorus of beings, humming truth, made stronger by and in community.

It's the same with witches. Because we know the God of many names, faces, and identities, because we know the God who is a communal force moving through the world in synchronized love, we, too, know the force, the power, the beauty of being together.

---

[26] Inspired by my actual friend, Sarah Jane Chapman, who is a body, mind, soul, and spirit healer through tarot, astrology, yoga therapy, and more.

[27] 1 Chronicles 10:13–14.

My abilities as a witch, in and of themselves, are strong; when Elohim, along with other witches and spirits, shows up, my abilities as a witch are unparalleled.

Remember, it's not that I see what others can't; it's that I see what others won't.

When we stop refusing to see the truth, any of us can become witches and messengers of God's truth. What a world that would be.

Amen.

* * *

A LITURGY FOR NIGHT PRAYER

OPENING

If you are gathered with others, position yourselves in a circle. Place a candle in the center, or, if you're feeling adventurous, make a fire, and practice this liturgy outside in a circle around it. If you are alone, light a candle (or make a fire) as a sign of connection to Mother God and to the circle of women who join you, even now, as you pray.

Opening Prayer at the Lighting of the Candles
(or at the making and tending of the fire)

> May the light of Elohim shine upon us.
>
> **May the truth of Elohim bless us and keep us.**
>
> May the face of Elohim grace us with wisdom and presence.
>
> **May Elohim's names and faces surround us with peace. Amen.**

Prayer of Confession and Accountability

> We confess to You, O God, and in the presence of one another, that we ban what we fear, ignore Your truth, bury Your love, and diminish Your presence, particularly when we fail to recognize these in others. How easy it is to

demean and villainize another person, forgetting they are your beloved child, too. Forgive us for fearing that which we do not understand. Forgive us for our attempts to erase mystery from our lives. Help us, O God, to practice curiosity, openness, and love. Help us, O God, to embrace the dark that we may come to see the light. In You, O God, we are redeemed and forever loved. Alleluia! Amen.

Psalm 59 (inspired by NRSV translation of the Bible)

Deliver us from our fears.

Protect us from our ignorance.

When we feel threatened, help us pause before taking action.

Keep us from reacting too quickly to that which confounds us and from doing harm in the name of healing.

You, O God, speak through the unlikely ones.

The bellowing of witches is divine.

Your Love greets us no matter how terrified we are.

Your Love begs us to lay our weapons down.

Therefore, we will sing of Your Love forever.

We will join with the women who sing truth.

Resting in Your coven of Love, we will open our hearts.

Resting in Your coven of Grace, we will reach out our hands and discover that we are not alone. Amen.

Scripture Reading: 1 Samuel 28: 3–25

A living, breathing word.

Thanks be to God.

Hold quiet for prayer and reflection.

Song of Praise

In the Beginning

Claire K. McKeever-Burgett

Contemporary Connection

Take a few moments to listen to "Season of the Witch" by Lana Del Rey.[28] *Imagine Eliora singing this song as Saul and his friends arrive at her coven-cave. Invite the rhythm and the melody to move in you and through you. Invite your friends to sing along (and, perhaps, dance along) with you. Welcome this song into your prayerful, worshipful, songful life.*

The Prayer of the Women

Holy Mother of sand and sea,

to You all honor and praise.

When we cry out, You hear us.

When we ask for help, You help us.

When we long to be loved, You love us.

May mercy be offered to everyone.

May power and dominion over others cease.

May greed and violence end.

---

[28] McKeever-Burgett, Claire, *Music for Contemporary Connections,* https://www.clairemckeeverburgett.com/*music, accessed July 10, 2025.*

May love live forever.

Birth us into a new world.

Help us make this one beautiful.

Stir us up. Settle us down.

Burn. Simmer. Refine.

When all else shakes, hold us steady.

When everyone else wants to blame,

remind us that in You there is only Love.

Our praise and our prayers are Yours, forever. Amen.

Closing Blessing

Hear the good news, beloveds: witches can be diviners of God's wisdom and grace. When we stop pretending to be something other than who we are, when we start telling the truth to ourselves, we connect with our inner witchiness, which is power, which is presence, which is love. Go, be open, be kind, be honest, be a witch. **Amen.**

REFLECTION QUESTIONS

The following questions are meant to deepen and expand, invite and beckon thoughtful, compassionate, and curious responses to the story and liturgy of Eliora. Whether considering these questions on your own or in a group setting, create space for journaling, collaging, or painting in response. If engaging in group discussion, choose one or two questions, at most, to hold at the center of your sacred circle.

1. What resonates with you about Eliora's story? What feels redemptive? What feels challenging?
2. When reading and praying with Eliora, Mother God, and the women, what sensations do you notice in your body?
3. What narratives about witches do you need to reconsider or rewrite in light of Eliora's story?
4. What qualities of Eliora do you want or need in your life?

PUBLIC WITNESS

Because what good are our prayers on Sunday if they make no meaning in our lives on Monday?

Part of our calling as people who claim to follow a God of love, justice , and mercy is to connect what we pray, sing, and hear on Sundays (or the day we set aside to worship God) to the whole of our lives. How does what we pray one day affect where we spend our time and financial resources on another day? How does praying for, about, and with women affect how we vote and whom we serve? God's loving call in Deuteronomy 6:5, "You shall love the Lord your God with all your heart, all your soul, and all your strength," commands us to integrate our faith into every aspect of our lives, which includes bearing witness to the good, necessary, and powerful work of justice-seeking, beauty-creating, love-making women in the world today.

Eliora made me think of all the women throughout time who've been punished for telling the truth. While Eliora is not explicitly punished in this story (though she is blamed for Saul's death), she and her kind have been banned by Saul himself, and she *does* deliver news that Saul does not want to hear, which puts her at risk. Dr. Christine Blasey Ford and Anita Hill are two women in American society who've been "burned at the stake" for telling the truth. They channel Eliora's spirit, as do the organizations and tools offered in their names.

The **Dr. Christine Blasey Ford Grant** with the **American Psychological Foundation** supports graduate students and early career researchers conducting innovative work focusing on the understanding, prevention, and/or treatment of the consequences of exposure to traumatic events such as sexual assault, sexual harassment, and/or rape. The **National Organization of Women Anita Hill and Sexual Harassment at Work Social Media Kit** includes sample tweets, hashtags, Facebook posts, and graphics to support the release of the documentary "Anita," creates dialogue about sexual harassment in the workplace, and educates people about what sexual harassment at work is and what one's legal rights surrounding it are.

Learn more about these organizations. Continue to support groups in your own communities that support women's voices, truths, stories, and lives. Connect. Learn. Give. Grow.[29]

[29] McKeever-Burgett, Claire, *Public Witness Woman-Led Nonprofits, https://www.clairemckeeverburgett.com/public-witness, accessed July 10, 2025.*

Chapter Eleven

Queen Vashti

Dissenter | Esther 1:10–16, 19–22

Vashti (name): of Persian origin meaning "beautiful" or "good"

* * *

On the seventh day, when the king was merry with wine, he commanded Mehuman, Biztha, Harbona, Bigtha and Abagtha, Zethar and Carkas, the seven eunuchs who attended him, to bring Queen Vashti before the king wearing the royal crown, in order to show the peoples and the officials her beauty, for she was fair to behold. But Queen Vashti refused to come at the king's command conveyed by the eunuchs. At this the king was enraged, and his anger burned within him.

Then the king consulted the sages who knew the laws (for this was the king's procedure toward all who were versed in law and custom, and those next to him were Carshena, Shethar, Admatha, Tarshish, Meres, Marsena, and Memucan, the seven officials of Persia and Media who had access to the king and sat first in the kingdom): "According to the law, what is to be done with Queen Vashti because she has not performed the command of King Ahasuerus conveyed by the eunuchs?" Then Memucan said in the presence of the king and the officials, "Queen Vashti has done wrong not only to the king but also to all the officials and all the peoples who are in all the provinces of King Ahasuerus.

Then Memucan said in the presence of the king and the officials… "If it pleases the king, let a royal order go out from him, and let it be written among the laws of the Persians and the Medes so that it may not be altered, that Vashti is never again to come before King Ahasuerus; and let the king give her royal position to another who is better than she. So when the decree made by the king is proclaimed throughout all his kingdom, vast as it is, all women will give honor to their husbands, high and low alike."

This advice pleased the king and the officials, and the king did as Memucan proposed; he sent letters to all the royal provinces, to every province in its own script and to every people in its own language, declaring that every man should be master in his own house.

—Esther 1:10–16, 19–22

* * *

QUEEN VASHTI'S STORY

I shake my head and sigh remembering the things the king demanded of me when I was queen. I try to push the memories out of my mind. Even when I succeed at pretending that the humiliating and degrading acts never happened, my body remembers. A subtle ache in my chest grows. A wave of sickness plagues my stomach. Tight hips radiate pain down my backside.

I compromised my values, my body, and my soul for far too long with King Ahasuerus, and I will die destitute and alone before I will return to him. The prospect of hunger and death feels like a warm hug compared to thoughts of living under his evil eye again.

Young and naive when my father submitted me as a prospect for queen, I thought this was finally my chance to demonstrate what I always knew was true: that I was beautiful and therefore fit for royalty. I was meant to bathe in luxurious oils and be dressed in the finest robes and jewels. I was meant to have people serve me. I was destined for greatness and queendom. Or so I thought.

Little did I know that the gleam of sitting in the lap of luxury would wane. No one told me that along with the glitz and glamour would also come sexual demands and abuse. No one prepared me for forced sexual intercourse or male domination. My mother and father were too enamored by the king's power and influence, mesmerized by his promises that I would be cared for and empowered as they believed all queens were, to see the truth.

I try not to blame them for their idiocy and ignorance. Surely my mother, at the very least, knew what I'd be forced to do. Though my father was no king, he was wealthy and powerful, made more so by keeping my beautiful mother by his side. Did he, too, force her to do things she didn't want to do? Or, even worse, did she convince herself she wanted to do them? That it was her duty to protect and obey my father at all costs?

I'm not here to go into detail about what was required of me as queen. It's far too traumatic to recount. Heartbreakingly, my guess is that you can imagine given your own trauma or your own awareness of what it's like to be a woman living in a man's world. I grieve for all of us who suffer at the hands of patriarchy, and I celebrate those of us who keep fighting against it, no matter what we've done to perpetuate it in the past. Surely the mercy of God extends to all of us.

* * *

On the fateful night that is recorded in the Book of Esther, when the king summons me to parade in front of his advisors wearing the royal crown, I sit, peacefully, in a sacred circle of women. For quite some time, we'd been creating safety and love for ourselves among the women of the palace. It was quite easy to do under the guise of offering royal banquets for the women of the royal home at the same time the king offered banquets for the men. Hosting these royal dinners was thought to be part of my role as queen, and I was happy to play along.

However, instead of drinking ourselves silly at these feasts, we shared our stories and sought one another's comfort. We held one another close. We sang. We prayed. And we began to heal. For some of us, healing looked like being honest about our anger, throwing things into the fire, screaming as a release. For others, healing meant finally allowing ourselves to cry.

* * *

We hear the footsteps of the men sent to collect me that night as Abigail shares her story. Quickly, as we are prepared to do, we take our goblets of wine, begin to drink, laugh, and play music. The men enter without knocking, taking their time to survey us. Up and down their eyes move along our bodies, like we are cattle they need for a sacrifice.

In my most pleasant, measured voice, I say, "To what do we owe the honor of your presence?"

Mehuman speaks first. "The king demands that you adorn the royal crown on your head and parade in front of us tonight."

He pauses. A thin-lipped smile smile slides its way across his face.

"Naked," he sneers.

This isn't the first time this request has been made of me. And, yes, I've paraded naked in front of the king and his men before. Tonight feels different. Tonight, it's as if a large boulder rolls its way down the mountain toward me, and I can either let it barrel into me, or I can move out of its way and let it bowl into something else.

Because I do not answer and react immediately, Mehuman speaks again. "The king demands that you wear the royal crown on your head and nothing else. He wants you parading naked for all of us to see."

The pleasure on Mehuman's face as he delivers the message sends shivers up my spine. The other messengers of the king laugh. Women are a joke to them.

However, women are not a joke to me, and I am not a joke to the ones witnessing this scene. In fact, it is the presence of the other women who give me the courage to refuse. Abigail, a woman who's become more than a friend to me, a woman I love and who loves me, reaches toward me and offers me her hand. I take it, and she rises to stand next to me, shoulders back, feet on the ground.

"No," I say to Mehuman, meeting his eyes with my own meditative stare.

"Excuse me?" he gasps. "What do you mean 'no'?"

"I will not go," I say. "I will not wear the crown, and I will not take off my clothes for the king or for any of you. I'm done playing his drunken, foolish games, and all of you should be, too. These demands he places on all of us are killing us, slowly but surely. I said no, and I mean no."

Flabbergasted, the men leave, but before Mehuman exits the room, he turns to me and says, "You'll be sorry."

The door slams, and we are alone again, for how long, I do not know. There's no telling what King Ahasuerus will do. Mercurial and mean, he is a beast of a man.

Abigail takes me in her arms and holds me. The other women begin to clap and pump their fists, whooping and hollering for all to hear.

When their celebrations settle, we each take one another's hands, reforming our sacred circle.

No is a full sentence! we say. *No can be just as holy a prayer as a yes can be. Amen and Amen.*

* * *

There are consequences for my actions, for sure. I am dethroned and am told I may never come before King Ahasuerus again. What they think is punishment is my pathway to freedom. What a gift it is to never be in the king's presence again. Finally, I am able to live life the way I want, liberated from the king's and other's expectations of me.

* * *

Abigail reaches for my hand. I've been staring out the window for some time now. We live in a small home with dirt floors. It's not much, but it's ours.

"What are you thinking about?" she asks.

"Oh, everything and nothing," I answer.

"Do you miss living in luxury?" Abigail asks, her voice breaking.

Turning toward her, I say, "Of course not!"

"Okay," she says long and slow, like she's taking her time to believe me. "It's just that we went from marbled floors to dirt ones in no time."

"Do *you* miss it?" I ask her.

"Sometimes, yes," she answers. "I don't miss the terror or the control, but I miss the luxury, for sure."

Her honesty has always been the thing I've loved most about her.

Pulling her close to me, we hold each other for a long time. Finally, I whisper in her ear, "Saying 'no' was the most sacred sentence I ever uttered."

Remaining close, she says, "I know."

We embrace for a long time in front of the window. A small tap of a bird's beak on the wooden abode shakes us from our closeness. Looking toward the sound, we see a small dove peering in at us. The dove's beady, black eyes stare at us, and we stare back. Before she flies to find her next meal, she taps the wood one more time and seems to nod our way. Like a blessing, like a peace note, like a prayer.

We smile, watching the small creature fly away. We squeeze each other's hands. We know, without saying another word, that no amount of luxury can replace what we have together in this small, dirt-floor home we've made and are making together. It is a safe haven, its own kind of luxury. To live as we want to live, together.

* * *

Abigail and I grow old together. We continue to circle up with other women, celebrating the sacred 'yes' and the sacred 'no.' We continue to live simply, learning to give thanks for the dirt floors that keep us bound to the truth. We continue to pray for women, everywhere:

That they may find the freedom to inhabit their skin fully for themselves and no one else.

That they may find other women with whom they feel safe, loved, and healed.

That they may find the courage within themselves to say "No" and to mean it, trusting that the courage comes from within *and* from the women lovers and friends who stand beside them, holding their hands and cheering them on.

That when they feel trapped and alone, when they know not what they do and when they know what they do and keep doing it, they will know that they are still worth loving.

* * *

Time and its passing made me wiser. Women and their presence made me whole again. Saying 'no' made me stronger. Leaving men who stood against my thriving made me free.

As for Esther, the queen who came after me, she, too, found her way to be both cunning and clever, usurping the king's dominion and saving her people. Though Esther did it differently than me, she, too, defied the king's law. Both of us confronted powerful men and the systems they created, uttering a sacred 'no' as a quiet prayer for ourselves and women everywhere.

Turns out a 'no' can be holy. Turns out revolutions can be quiet. Turns out women have been softly moving toward the truth and power within us forever.

May it continue to be so. Amen.

LITURGY FOR MORNING PRAYER

If you are gathered with others, position yourselves in a circle. Place a lit candle in the center. If you are alone, light a candle as a sign of connection to Mother God and to the women who join you, even here, even now as you pray.

Morning Confession

Saying 'no' can be a sacred act.

Blessed are the women who say 'no.'

Morning Prayer of Gratitude

For the women who, throughout time, have said 'no,'
saving themselves and others from harm, we give thanks.

For the women who, throughout time, have held one another's hands and stood alongside one another in love, we give thanks.

For women's connection, wisdom, mercy, and love today
and always, we give thanks.

Morning Psalm | Psalm 90: 14–17
(inspired by the Common English Bible translation)

Every morning, no matter where we wake, your love is
with us and for us.

Therefore, we rejoice and celebrate together forever.

Show us true expressions of joy now that we are free from years of male power, abuse, and affliction.

May your love be known by all.

May your protection be known by our daughters.

May the kindness of God be within us

so that as we hold one another's hands,

our work to seek justice, mercy, and love will last. **Amen.**

Scripture Reading: Esther 1

A word by which to learn. **Thanks be to God.**

Silence for prayer and reflection.

Prayers for Women who say 'No'

For women who say 'no' in a world that demands they say 'yes,' we pray.

For their strength, wisdom, and courage,

For loving companions to join them on the way,

For safe places to heal,

For loving places to grow,

For sunshine to warm,

For moonshine to inspire,

For freedom in mind, body, and spirit,

For a world in which violent, humiliating demands are no longer required of anyone,

we pray with our whole minds, hearts, souls, and bodies in the name of Holy Wisdom Herself.

Amen.

Song of Praise

In the Beginning

Claire K. McKeever-Burgett

Contemporary Connection

Take a few moments to listen to "fake smile" by Ariana Grande.[30] *Imagine Vashti singing this song as she proclaims her sacred "no." Invite this song into your prayerful, worshipful, songful life.*

The Prayer of the Women

Holy Mother of sand and sea,

to You all honor and praise.

When we cry out, You hear us.

When we ask for help, You help us.

When we long to be loved, You love us.

May mercy be offered to everyone.

---

[30] McKeever-Burgett, Claire, *Music for Contemporary Connections,* https://www.clairemckeeverburgett.com/*music, accessed July 10, 2025.* (Please note that this song uses some strong language that some may find offensive. My intention in including this song is to show how strong language can be a way to reclaim what feels right and true and good to you, as well to release what does not. If the use of strong language might distract or detract from your morning prayer experience, please listen to the edited version of the song on the Spotify playlist included at the end of the book.)

May power and dominion over others cease.
May greed and violence end.
May love live forever.
Birth us into a new world.
Help us make this one beautiful.
Stir us up. Settle us down.
Burn. Simmer. Refine.
When all else shakes, hold us steady.
When everyone else wants to blame,
remind us that in You there is only Love.
Our praise and our prayers are Yours, forever. Amen.

REFLECTION QUESTIONS

The following questions are meant to deepen and expand, invite and beckon thoughtful, compassionate, and curious responses to the story and liturgy of Queen Vashti. Whether considering these questions on your own or in a group setting, create space for journaling, collaging, or painting in response. If engaging in group discussion, choose one or two questions, at most, to hold at the center of your sacred circle.

1. What resonates with you about Queen Vashti's story? What feels redemptive? What feels challenging?
2. When reading and praying with Queen Vashti, Mother God, and the women, what sensations do you notice in your body?
3. When have you wanted to utter a sacred 'no' but haven't? When did you utter a sacred 'no,' and why?
4. What qualities of Queen Vashti do you want or need in your life?

PUBLIC WITNESS

Because what good are our prayers on Sunday if they make no meaning in our lives on Monday?

Part of our calling as people who claim to follow a God of love, justice, and mercy is to connect what we pray, sing, and hear on

Sundays (or the day we set aside to worship God) to the whole of our lives. How does what we pray one day affect where we spend our time and financial resources on another day? How does praying for, about, and with women affect how we vote and whom we serve? God's loving call in Deuteronomy 6:5, "You shall love the Lord your God with all your heart, all your soul, and all your strength," commands us to integrate our faith into every aspect of our lives, which includes bearing witness to the good, necessary, and powerful work of justice-seeking, beauty-creating, love-making women in the world today.

I cannot read Vashti's story of sacred refusal without thinking of Simone Biles, the most decorated gymnast in history, who, during the 2021 Olympic Games withdrew from competing (essentially saying "no" to parading in front of the world) to protect her mental and physical health. For this reason and connection, I highlight **Friends of the Children**, a nonprofit near and dear to Biles' work and heart, as well as **Strong Girls United Foundation**, which focuses on women's and girls' mental health in sports.

Friends of the Children creates generational change by empowering youth who face the greatest obstacles by offering them relationships with professional mentors. **Friends of the Children** is committed to diversity, equity, inclusion, justice, belonging, and liberation. Its goal is for every child to know and feel that they truly belong. Simone Biles knows from her own experience in foster care that children face a lot of hard things growing up, which is why she's a fierce advocate for **Friends of the Children** and the power of mentoring to create transformational change in the lives of youth and children across the United States.

Strong Girls United Foundation empowers girls and women to be **strong, confident**, and **resilient** through sports, mentorship, and mental health programming. The foundation pursues this mission by inspiring girls through programs led by female role models, evidence-based curriculum that teaches mental health and mental skills, trauma-informed and culturally responsive mentoring, and physical activity, sport, and play to remind all girls and young women of the fun inherent in sports.[31]

[31] McKeever-Burgett, Claire, *Public Witness Woman-Led Nonprofits, https://www.clairemckeeverburgett.com/public-witness, accessed July 10, 2025.*

Learn more about these organizations. Continue to support groups in your own communities that promote mentorship and support of vulnerable children, as well as the mental health of girls and young women who play sports. Connect. Learn. Give. Grow.

Chapter Twelve

Chokmah

Justice Seeker | Proverbs 1:20–33 and 8:22–36

Chokmah (name): of Hebrew origin meaning "wisdom"

* * *

Out in the open, wisdom calls aloud,
She raises her voice in the public square;
on top of the wall she cries out,
at the city gate she makes her speech:
"How long will you, who are ignorant, love your ignorant ways?
How long will mockers delight in mockery
and fools hate knowledge?

Repent!

Then I will pour out my thoughts to you,
I will make known to you my teachings.
But since you refuse to listen when I call
and no one pays attention when I stretch out my hand,
since you disregard all my advice
and do not accept my rebuke,
I in turn will laugh when disaster strikes you;
I will mock when calamity overtakes you—
For the waywardness of the ignorant will kill them,
and the complacency of fools will destroy them;
but whoever listens to me will live in safety
and be at ease, without fear of harm."

—Proverbs 1:20–33 adapted from New International Version (NIV)

"The LORD brought me forth as the first of Her works,
before Her deeds of old;
I was formed long ages ago,
at the very beginning, when the world came to be.
When there were no watery depths, I was given birth,
when there were no springs overflowing with water;
before the mountains were settled in place,
before the hills, I was given birth,
before God made the world or its fields
or any of the dust of the earth.
I was there when God set the heavens in place,
when God marked out the horizon on the face of the deep,
Then I was constantly at God's side.
I was filled with delight day after day,
rejoicing always in God's presence,
rejoicing in God's whole world
and delighting in humankind.

"Now then, my children, listen to me;
blessed are those who keep my ways.
Listen to my instruction and be wise;
do not disregard it.
Blessed are those who listen to me,
watching daily at my doors,
waiting at my doorway.
For those who find me find life
and receive favor from the LORD.
But those who fail to find me harm themselves."

— Proverbs 8:22–36 adapted from New International Version (NIV)

* * *

CHOKMAH'S STORY

It was a time of plenty for a few and of little for the multitudes. The ones with plenty made weapons of war and used them. The ones with little built bunkers and tried to hide.

Many died. Many were injured. Many cried out in sorrow and pain, echoing the Psalmists' cry, "How long, O Lord! How long?"[32]

It was a time when the rich got richer and the poor got poorer, when wayward men led wayward people down a deep, dark hole of foolishness and ignorance.

With nowhere to go, many people slept on the streets. Many had to move to ensure the safety of themselves and their families. Many cried out, "Do they not know what they do?"

It was a time when the ones in power knew exactly what they were doing and who they were hurting, and they didn't care. Women were reduced to the functions of their bodies. Men were reduced to agents of domination and control. Everyone was in pain, whether they knew it or not.

* * *

I awake from my slumber with a shake of my head.

Looking to Holy Mother God, who rests to my right, I say, "I had a dream that the world and its people were at war. That resources were scarce, and very few people, if any, were following Wisdom's way."

"Sadly, it is not a dream," Holy Mother says back to me.

"What do you mean?" I ask in response.

"I mean that your dream is reality," Holy Mother replies.

"Is it time to go?" I ask.

"Yes," She says.

Packing a satchel that I can easily throw over my shoulder, I tie my sandals and set out for earth.

* * *

The mother's wails are the first tell. The lack of children's laughter is the second. A wasteland of boarded, abandoned houses and businesses, the third.

---

[32] Psalm 13:1.

A ghost town exists in the valley, but a rally in the city. The juxtaposition couldn't be more stark.

The city stands high on a hill, adorned in white and gold. Lavishly dressed people sit in their marbled fortresses, eating and drinking until their stomachs are full. A pulsating beat shakes the ground as I walk upon it.

* * *

On the steps of the largest building in the city stands someone who appears to be a ruler, flanked by his guards. Teeming crowds of men stand on the ground below, looking up, hanging on the ruler's every move and word.

I am wearing a purple robe and a multicolored headscarf that my grandmother sewed for me when I became a woman.

Pushing my way through the crowd, I arrive at the bottom of the steps where I can hear the ruler's words more clearly.

We only want our kind here! We will take back what is ours!

The ruler shouts, spit flying from his mouth; the crowd pulsates with glee.

We will do what we want, when we want it! We will be great again!

On the edges of the crowd stand women, a few men, some children, and those who identify as none of these labels, the beautifully gender nonconforming, the holy other. They stand with their backs to the ruler and the throng. My eyes follow their bodies around the city center, which they encircle. They are not here for the rally. They are not here to make themselves great again. (I can tell they already know they are great and need no ruler to tell them so). They are here to protest fear and hate. They are here to hold vigil for all those the ruler seeks to harm.

I am here to join them and to give voice to their cries. I am here to deliver a message from Holy Mother God.

* * *

Bounding up the steps, I stand a few feet in front of the ruler and begin to speak.

"To anyone who can hear, listen!" I shout.

For a moment, the beat of the music drowns my voice. The people, mesmerized by their glut, do not hear me.

Again, I yell, "To anyone who can hear, listen!"

The ruler's guards lunge toward me. I nimbly climb high on a platform, evading their grasp. I continue to speak.

"How long will you ignore the truth? How long will you despise what is honest?"

Get the bitch out of here! they scream. *Burn her at the stake!*

"Heed my call. Follow me. And I will make my thoughts and wisdom known to you."

What does a woman know? they jeer. *Shut your mouth, dog.*

The ruler regains his composure and, to control his angry pack, shouts, "Let her speak. She's just a woman. What harm can she possibly cause?"

At this precise moment, the holy members of the circle turn their bodies in unison toward the steps and toward me. Coordinated with every move, they lift their chins, and they begin to hum.

A slow, deep hum grows into a loud vibration. So loud, it quiets the army's drumbeat and overcomes the men's yells. It is almost as if they are a pod of whales foraging for food on the ocean floor, vocalizing through groans, moans, roars, and sighing that they aren't going anywhere until their bellies are full.

One of the women, who appears to be their leader, subtly nods her head toward me as if to say, *Continue.* And so, I do.

"When you refuse to listen to me," I proclaim, "When you refuse to follow me, when you mock the very integrity upon which the world was born, when you defile women and ignore the poor, I will be with the women and the poor, singing. You will call upon me, and I will not answer because I'll have sweet music in my ears. You will seek me diligently, but you will not find me because I will be dancing in joy."

The swarm of men begins to break. They are disaffected by my words. They even push a few women to the ground as they leave. The ruler and his guards discount my words. They return to their plush homes and palaces, impenetrable to the brokenhearted cries rising from the valley.

The circle of the faithful, however, remain. They invite me into the center.

Tell us more, they beg. *Tell us: Who are you? Where do you come from?*

"I am Holy Wisdom, and I come from Holy Mother God, just like each of you. There in the very beginning, before the light and the dark and the trees and the ground were made, Holy Mother gave birth to me. I was by Her side when the heavens formed. I was with Her constantly, and it was the joy of my soul."

What is required of us to live in peace? What will become of the ones who do not listen to you?

"Seek the wisdom that is inside of you. Listen to me, and you will be blessed. Honor one another. Feed the poor. Tend the sick. Clothe the naked. Love what is right in front of you, here and now. Let what wants to die, die. Give birth to the beauty that wants to be born. We have so little control over anything other than the love we can give ourselves and those around us. This, though not a cure all, will bring peace. Loved ones, live with integrity and you will become the very things for which you long."

Before we leave the steps of worldly power, I approach every person in the circle, place my hands upon their heads, and say, "You are loved. You are wise. Be at peace."

Then, taking my place in the center of the circle, they extend their hands and hearts toward me, singing, "You are loved. You are wise. Be at peace."

* * *

My name is Chokmah. I am Woman Wisdom, and I came not to solve the world's problems with external answers, but to point people back to themselves. The wise ones look inward. They keep things simple and small. They love those whom they can touch, whom they can see. They feed those whom they can feed.

This is how the world heals. Not all at once. Slowly, one person, one circle, one blessing, one song, one birth, one meal, one woman at a time.

In times of plenty and in times of little, in times of wealth and in times of destitution, the wise ones know to keep small and close. The wise ones know their wisdom lies within and that therefore no ruler, no mob of men, no economic policy or political parade can take from them what is theirs. The wise ones know that new worlds are always being made. The wise ones know to find the women, circled up and singing.

Amen.

LITURGY FOR EVENING PRAYER

Gather in a circle with a candle at the center. Light the candle. Breathe. Enter this sacred time with quiet and ease, trusting Woman Wisdom and Holy Mother God who gave birth to Her are with you, even here, even now, as you pray.

Evening Prayer

We give thanks for this moment of quiet
at the end of our day—
Sacred time to reflect, pray, and to be with ourselves,
one another, and God.
Every wise decision we made today,
Every foolish one,
Every ambiguous thought and feeling,
Every decisive one,

We give to You, O God and Your Infinite Wisdom.

Woman Wisdom has been with You

from the very beginning, and She is with us now.

We open our hearts, minds, bodies, and spirits

to what She has to say and what she must reveal.

May we hear. May we see. Amen.

Psalm 1 (inspired by the Common English Bible)

Blessed are the women who seek Wisdom and Her ways.

Blessed are the ones, no matter their identities, who delight

in the Love of God and who stand with the least and the last

anytime, anywhere, calling for justice, mercy, and peace.

These faithful ones are like trees planted by flowing streams. They yield goodness for Mercy's sake and for the sake of all in harm's way.

But the ones who do not follow Wisdom—

who scoff at those standing in circles singing,

who ignore the truth and live in folly,

who wreak havoc wherever they go—

those ones will wither away.

Therefore, hear the good news:

those who gloat over us,

those who make laws that harm us,

those who distort the Love of God

are not our final judges.

Holy Mother and Her Wisdom offer final judgment,

Holy Mother and Her Wisdom are with us,

leading us to righteousness and love.

The wayward ones harm themselves.

Though they do not see it,
they lead themselves to their
own destruction and demise.

Scripture Reading: Proverbs 1: 20–33 and Proverbs 8: 22–36

Holy Wisdom cries out for us to hear! **Thanks be to God!**

A moment of quiet for prayer and reflection.

The Prayers of the People

If gathered with a group of people, invite three different people to read the prayers of Wisdom, Whimsy, and Witness. If praying and worshipping alone read all the parts yourself.

Wisdom: For all who do not see the harm they create,

All: Open our eyes, hearts, and minds.

Whimsy: For all who do not realize the joy they steal,

All: Lead us beside still waters where we can splash and play.

Witness: For all who forget to bear witness to Love,

All: Show us what mercy and compassion look like in practice.

Wisdom: For the women who stand on the sidelines, singing,

All: May we join them in the everlasting song of love.

Whimsy: For the ones who hold steady in the truth of Woman Wisdom,

All: May we join them in their steadiness on the front lines of justice.

Witness: For the ones who proclaim the truth,

All: May we join them in doing the same. Amen.

Song of Praise

In the Beginning

Claire K. McKeever-Burgett

Contemporary Connection

Take a few moments to listen to and watch "Wise Woman" by Darcy Nelson and "Can't Catch Me Now" by Olivia Rodrigo.[33] *As you listen, imagine Chokmah and the women singing these songs together, standing in their wisdom and love. Invite the songs to be a part of your prayerful, worshipful, songful life.*

The Prayer of the Women

Holy Mother of sand and sea,
to You all honor and praise.
When we cry out, You hear us.
When we ask for help, You help us.
When we long to be loved, You love us.
May mercy be offered to everyone.
May power and dominion over others cease.
May greed and violence end.
May love live forever.
Birth us into a new world.

[33] McKeever-Burgett, Claire, *Music for Contemporary Connections*, https://www.clairemckeeverburgett.com/*music, accessed July 10, 2025.*

Help us make this one beautiful.

Stir us up. Settle us down.

Burn. Simmer. Refine.

When all else shakes, hold us steady.

When everyone else wants to blame,

remind us that in You there is only Love.

Our praise and our prayers are Yours, forever. Amen.

Closing Blessing

You're invited to bless one another the way the Chokmah and the holy circle of people bless one another in the story. A leader or two can walk to each person in the circle and say, "You are Loved. You are Wise. Be at Peace," *or you can hold hands and say the blessing aloud together. If you are alone, place your hands on your forehead or heart and say the blessing to yourself: You are Loved. You are Wise. Be at Peace.*

REFLECTION QUESTIONS

The following questions are meant to deepen and expand, invite and beckon thoughtful, compassionate, and curious responses to the story and liturgy of Chokmah. Whether considering these questions on your own or in a group setting, create space for journaling, collaging, or painting in response. If engaging in group discussion, choose one or two questions, at most, to hold at the center of your sacred circle.

1. What resonates with you about Chokmah's story? What feels redemptive? What feels challenging?
2. When reading and praying with Chokmah, what sensations do you notice in your body?
3. Where do you see Woman Wisdom alive in your life? Where would you like to see Her more alive in your life?
4. What does your own inner wisdom, the wisdom that lives within you, look like and feel like today?

PUBLIC WITNESS

Because what good are our prayers on Sunday if they make no meaning in our lives on Monday?

Part of our calling as people who claim to follow a God of love, justice, and mercy is to connect what we pray, sing, and hear on Sundays (or the day we set aside to worship God) to the whole of our lives. How does what we pray one day affect where we spend our time and financial resources on another day? How does praying for, about, and with women affect how we vote and whom we serve? God's loving call in Deuteronomy 6:5, "You shall love the Lord your God with all your heart, all your soul, and all your strength," commands us to integrate our faith into every aspect of our lives, which includes bearing witness to the good, necessary, and powerful work of justice-seeking, beauty-creating, love-making women in the world today.

Chokmah speaks truth to power no matter how controversial or off-putting, understanding it as the call of Holy Mother God upon her life to embody and proclaim justice. The **Daughters of Wisdom** is a group of faithful women who, among many things, operate the **Wisdom House**, which is an interfaith retreat and conference center dedicated to spirituality, wellness, the arts, and ecology. **Daughters of Wisdom** practice nonviolence and are committed to seeking and contemplating divine wisdom in a world that hungers for meaning, justice, and compassion.

Learn more about this organization. Continue to support groups in your own communities that promote women's wisdom, leadership, justice, and love. Connect. Learn. Give. Grow.[34]

---

[34] McKeever-Burgett, Claire, *Public Witness Woman-Led Nonprofits, https://www.clairemckeeverburgett.com/public-witness, accessed July 10, 2025.*

Part Four

Warriors stand with their feet on the ground, their arms open wide, and their hearts on their sleeves, ready, at any moment, to protect themselves and those whom they love. Though the traditional understanding of warrior, especially in biblical times, meant a person engaged or experienced in warfare, women warriors are more akin to those who demonstrate vigor and courage in the face of daunting circumstances, of which there can be and are myriad. Additionally, as a yoga practitioner, I see women warriors standing in a strong pose, ready for whatever life requires of them.

Chapter Thirteen

Jael

Survivor | Judges 4:17–22 and 5:24–27

Jael (name): of Hebrew origin meaning "climber" or "she will go up"

Content Warning: Rape and Sexual Violence

* * *

Now Sisera had fled away on foot to the tent of Jael wife of Heber the Kenite, for there was peace between King Jabin of Hazor and the clan of Heber the Kenite. Jael came out to meet Sisera and said to him, "Turn aside, my lord, turn aside to me; have no fear." So he turned aside to her into the tent, and she covered him with a rug. Then he said to her, "Please give me a little water to drink, for I am thirsty." So she opened a skin of milk and gave him a drink and covered him. He said to her, "Stand at the entrance of the tent, and if anybody comes and asks you, 'Is anyone here?' say, 'No.'" But Jael wife of Heber took a tent peg and took a hammer in her hand and went softly to him and drove the peg into his temple, until it went down into the ground—he was lying fast asleep from weariness—and he died. Then, as Barak came in pursuit of Sisera, Jael went out to meet him and said to him, "Come, and I will show you the man whom you are seeking." So he went into her tent, and there was Sisera lying dead, with the tent peg in his temple.

—Judges 4:17–22

Most blessed of women be Jael,
the wife of Heber the Kenite,
of tent-dwelling women most blessed.
He asked water and she gave him milk,
she brought him curds in a lordly bowl.
She put her hand to the tent-peg
and her right hand to the workmen's mallet;

she struck Sisera a blow,
she crushed his head,
she shattered and pierced his temple.

He sank, he fell,
he lay still at her feet;
at her feet he sank, he fell;
where he sank, there he fell dead.

—Judges 5:24–27

* * *

JAEL'S STORY

War was always at our doorstep. Someone was always killing someone. Armies were always being formed. Land was always being conquered. People were always either victors or victims.

We women were often caught in the crossfire, pulled into men's wars whether we wanted it or not. We constantly had to make choices about our own and our children's safety. We constantly had to choose a side—us or them?

As for choosing ourselves? That choice didn't exist. As women we had no "self" apart from the position of our people.

From the very beginning, Eve's heart broke in two because of the war between her sons.

It doesn't have to be this way, she cried.

Of course, she was right. It didn't have to be that way—the violent, territorial, war-like way—but here we were, years later, still fighting the same war but with more people, more tribes, more conflicts, more territories.

My husband, Heber the Kenite, made peace with King Jabin as a political move to ensure our safety, but it was all smoke and mirrors. No one was safe if we valued the occupation of people and land over the actual people and land. If we thought of the earth as ours to own rather than ours to tend, we would find ourselves at war.

As Heber made "peace" with Jabin, I was busy making peace with myself. Doing the work to be honest about what I would stand for and what I wouldn't, learning to honor my boundaries—knowing deep down that I shared an ancient connection with our first mother, Eve. Her broken heart was my broken heart; my broken heart was hers.

* * *

After I killed Sisera, I learned of Deborah's prophecy saying as much. Of course, the men who got to tell Deborah's story and my own made it about shaming Barak for his cowardice because he was reluctant to go into battle. Therefore, because he was reluctant, Barak would be shamed by the fact that Sisera would fall at the hands of a woman instead of at the hands of Barak.

What breaks my heart more than anything is that Barak was gentle and nurturing but had to hide those qualities to live in our world. Men were supposed to be fierce, emotionally impenetrable warriors; women were the ones who were supposed to be gentle and kind, nurturing and soft.

For a man to act like a woman was one of the worst offenses; for a woman to act like a man was unheard of.

Yet, here we were, Barak, Deborah, and me, flipping the traditional gendered scripts on their heads. Deborah, prophesying Sisera's death, leading the Israelites into battle; Barak, reluctant and afraid; Me, willing to kill to save myself.

* * *

Deborah was right: Sisera *did* fall at the hands of a woman. My hands. Murderous ones unwilling to accept the sexual advances of Sisera, unwilling to die at the altar of his need for domination and control over me.

It is late when Sisera arrives, breathless and afraid.

"Help me," he cries.

Who do I look like, I think, *your mother?*

Instead of speaking my thoughts aloud, I reply, "What do you need?"

"Food, drink, a place to hide," he gasps.

"Here, drink this." I share a cup of goat's milk left over from dinner.

"Here, eat this." I extend my hand, full of bread.

He devours the bread; he gulps the milk.

I remain standing the entire time. Tense, on edge, hyper-aware of my surroundings, I don't trust him for a second not to turn on me.

Once he hydrates and eats, I hope he will fall asleep, exhausted from his escape. Instead, the food and water invigorate him. He seems to like the chase. "They can come and find me!" he yells. "Bring it on!" he screams to nothing and no one in particular.

I remain standing, unimpressed, yet extremely uneasy with his act of invulnerability.

He throws off his outer robe and takes off his shoes. My eyes cut his way ever so slightly.

"Where shall we lie?" he snarls.

"We?" I ask in return, an attempt to deflect his advance.

"Yes, we," he sneers.

Lunging toward me, his large, sweaty hands grab my lower back and pull me toward him. I shudder but try to soften, my survival instincts kicking into high gear.

His hot breath smells like rancid onion and animal's blood. It seeps down my neck.

"Here, here," I play along, "Lie here." Gesturing toward my bed, I invite him to lie down.

"Let me get you some wine."

I bring him a generous pour, and, like he's a child asking for Mother's milk, he opens his mouth. For a moment, I forget I'm trying to trick him, and I flood his mouth so quickly he begins to choke.

"Oh, I'm so sorry," I say.

"What are you trying to do?" he gasps. "Choke me?"

Laughing nervously, I reply, "Of course not, dear Sisera. I'm just excited."

He lies down, softening into the bed mat.

"Put down the cup," he commands.

Then, grabbing me, once again by the small of my back, he forces me toward him and begins kissing me, now with wine-soaked lips that make me shudder.

"My lord," I address him quietly, submissively. "I need to make sure my tent door is closed and secure. I wouldn't want anyone to find us here."

"Yes, yes, go quickly," he slurs.

On my way to the opening, I pray he passes out. I need a few moments to find a weapon.

Once at the threshold, I kneel down to secure its closing by driving pegs into the flap of the tent, attaching it to the ground. Taking a peg and the hammer that remains by the tent's opening for exactly this purpose, I drive the first peg into the ground, securing one side of the door.

"Hurry up, already," Sisera groans.

"I'll be there in a minute," I say, staving off his demand.

I take the other tent peg in my hand and swing the hammer toward its end a few times so that it makes the same sound as the other one. But I keep it in my shaking hand rather than plunging it into the ground.

"I'm on my way," I say to Sisera. He lies on my bed, his feet facing away from me, his head closest to the tent's door. He has disrobed completely, ready for me to join him.

Moving swiftly, I swing the hammer as hard as I can toward his head. His eyes roll back, and he begins to bleed. Then, I take the peg, place it on his forehead, and drive it into his skull. It takes seven swings, seven hits to drive it all the way through, his body flailing with each one.

It is brutal and violent, and my hot, salty tears fall down my face and onto his, mixing with the blood gushing from his head wound.

Bone-weary, I fall back from his dying body, gasping for air, and begin to scream.

* * *

The soldiers found me, sweaty, shaky, and screaming.

"What have you done?" they asked.

"He's dead," I cried. "He's dead."

When they realized it was Sisera, they took his body to the Israelites to celebrate conquering the enemy.

"What you prophesied came true," they said to Deborah. "Sisera fell at the hands of a woman."

* * *

After Sisera's body was removed from my tent, I ran to the riverbank to wash my hands and face of his stench and blood. Frantically, I brought the water again and again to my face, head, and hands. It wasn't enough.

Stripping every piece of clothing from my body, I immersed my whole self in the water.

When my head broke the water's surface, I took a deep breath and plunged back under. I did this repeatedly, hoping each time I emerged from the water, I'd feel something. Exhausted, I finally stopped, letting myself float.

That's when I heard them—the women warriors, walking toward me in the river, singing.

You do not carry this alone.

We are with you. God is with you.

Hallelu, hallelu, hallelujah.

One by one, they, too, took off their clothes and immersed themselves in the water alongside me.

I started to speak, though no words formed. One of the women, very old and wrinkled, gently lifted her palm and shook her head. "We need no explanation. We understand."

* * *

It's not that the waters absolved me of my sin, and I'm still a bit confused as to whether I sinned or not when I drove the peg into Sisera's head. It's that the waters helped me remember that I come from the infinite love of God, where women naturally join God and me, requiring no explanation, no long, dramatic story. Only presence. Only abiding. Only togetherness.

The truth is that I drove a peg into Sisera's skull not to save the Israelites but to save myself. For far too long men had enacted their wars on women's bodies, treating us as objects to be conquered and controlled, and I was done. No more. Not today. Not with me. No.

I chose myself over all else. Over my husband, Heber. Over Sisera's abhorrent desires. Even over the Israelites' need to win.

And choosing myself in that moment meant that the Israelite women were saved from being raped by the enemy. Choosing myself in that moment meant I saved countless other women.

Perhaps I justify the one murder because it prevented hundreds of them. With this, I daily make my peace.

* * *

Though Deborah and I never met face to face, we heard of one another through the voices of the women who sang our praises and gave thanks to God for us.

Deborah knew me through her prophecy, and I knew her through other women who told me of her power and who sang her song of victory.

Awake! Awake!

Arise! Arise!

Be a friend of the fire.

Turn your face toward the sun.

My face is wrinkled like a prune because of how often I've turned my face toward the sun, and because of how often I've then washed it in the river. Most days, the fire and the water are the only reprieves I have from the terror I've lived most of my life.

Both the sun and the water have emboldened and softened me, reminding me that to warm myself by the fire and to cleanse myself in the river are, perhaps, the most important things I can ever do in the reality of both life and death, both war and peace, both brutality and blessing.

In the end, we each must make a thousand different choices about a thousand different things in our lives. Some will be right, some will be wrong, most will be a mix of both. I beg you, dear ones, not to celebrate me, but also not to condemn me. I beg you to find a place in the sun or by the fire, close to the riverbank or lakeshore or beach. Let the warmth burn from you the need for clear-cut answers, and let the waters cleanse you of the posture of self-righteous indignation.

I am Jael, warrior woman and survivor. I release into the water all that must make its way to the sea where the forever love of God carries and holds it all so that we don't have to. Amen.

LITURGY FOR NIGHT PRAYER

OPENING

If you are gathered with others, position yourselves in a circle. Place a lit candle and basin of water in the center. If you are alone, light a candle and pour a basin or bowl of water as a sign of connection to Mother God and to the circle of women who join you, even here, even now, as you pray.

Opening Prayer at the Lighting of the Candles and the Pouring of the Water

Into the hands of our Creator, we give the uncertainty and complexity of today. **Amen.**

With curiosity and love, we sit around the fire and the water with our God, listening and softening to love. **Amen.**

We release every moment of this day into the Flame of Love and the Waters of Togetherness, trusting that we are not alone in what we carry. **Amen.**

From the sun's rising to its setting, our God is with us, forming, forgiving, and befriending. **Amen.**

Prayer of Confession

Take a piece of paper and write on it something from which you long to be free. Holding the paper in the palms of your hands, give yourself time and space to breathe. Confess what needs confessing. Ask what needs asking. Release what needs releasing.

As you breathe with the paper in your hands, ask yourself:

Who are the women who've joined me in the waters of my fear and despair to remind me that I am not alone?

In what systems of violence and subjugation of women am I complicit?

What can I release that might bring about deeper healing and wider love?

After breathing deeply with these questions and after bringing your truth before God, pray this prayer:

God, you join us in the reality of our lives, seeing us and life both as it is and as it could be. Though our vision is limited, our wars are many, and our systems are complex; though we complicate your Love and often cause our own and others' suffering, You never leave us.

Show us the way to the Fire of Mercy. Be for us the Flame of Love. Invite us into the Waters of Healing. Stir in us the longing for wholeness, and, with your help, set us free.

May violence within and without cease. May shame within and without end. May joy, peace, safety, and love reign within us and among us forevermore, we pray. Amen.

PSALM 4 (inspired by the Common English Bible translation.)

Release the piece of paper into the fire or into the water, let it burn or dissolve. Let it rest. Let it be free, so that you can be free, too.

You answer us, Loving Flame, Holy Water, in the light of the sun and in the clarity of the waters.

Our troubles are many, and of those we have brought many upon ourselves and the women upon whose bodies we fight our wars.

Hear us and forgive us, we pray!

Show us the beauty of all creation.

Lead us away from dominance and control.

May this be our faithful witness—to follow peace, justice, and love.

May this be our faithful witness—to advocate for women and the actions that will support their healing, surviving, and thriving.

We know God takes care of those relegated to the margins.

They are the faithful ones, and God sees them and loves them.

If the light of God's face cannot be seen, it is time to repent.

If the waters of God's love cannot be felt, it is time to rediscover communities of love and accountability.

It is time to release what no longer serves the world God loves.

When we let go of our need for dominance and control,

when we learn to live alongside all of God's good creation,

our hearts fill with joy.

Then, we can sleep in peace

because God and the women protect us.

Amen.

Hold space for quiet to meditate on the Psalm.

Scripture Reading: Judges 4:17–22 and 5:24–27

A living word. **Thanks be to God.**

Hold space for quiet to meditate on the Scripture reading.

Communal Response

Tonight, we will rest in the fire of knowing

that you, O God, shine on us and in us,

leading us to repentance and freedom.

Amen.

Song of Praise

Contemporary Connection

Take a few moments to watch and listen to "Warrior" by Heather Mae.[35] *Imagine Jael singing this song before the shining sun and before the burning fire. Invite this song into your prayerful, worshipful, songful life.*

The Prayer of the Women

Holy Mother of sand and sea,

to You all honor and praise.

When we cry out, You hear us.

When we ask for help, You help us.

---

[35] McKeever-Burgett, Claire, *Music for Contemporary Connections,* https://www.clairemckeeverburgett.com/*music, accessed July 10, 2025.*

When we long to be loved, You love us.

May mercy be offered to everyone.

May power and dominion over others cease.

May greed and violence end.

May love live forever.

Birth us into a new world.

Help us make this one beautiful.

Stir us up. Settle us down.

Burn. Simmer. Refine.

When all else shakes, hold us steady.

When everyone else wants to blame,

remind us that in You there is only Love.

Our praise and our prayers are Yours, forever. Amen.

Closing Blessing

When we accept ambiguity and nuance, we can grow. When we sit with survivors, we can learn. When we love, we can be free. May it ever be so. Amen.

REFLECTION QUESTIONS

The following questions are meant to deepen and expand, invite and beckon thoughtful, compassionate, and curious responses to the story and liturgy of Jael. Whether considering these questions on your own or in a group setting, create space for journaling, collaging, or painting in response. If engaging in group discussion, choose one or two questions, at most, to hold at the center of your sacred circle.

1. What resonates with you about Jael's story? What feels redemptive? What feels challenging?
2. When reading and praying with Jael, what sensations do you notice in your body?
3. What does *survivor* mean to you?
4. What does *warrior* mean to you?

5. Who in your life joins you in the clear waters to remind you that you are not alone?

PUBLIC WITNESS

Because what good are our prayers on Sunday if they make no meaning in our lives on Monday?

Part of our calling as people who claim to follow a God of love, justice, and mercy is to connect what we pray, sing, and hear on Sundays (or the day we set aside to worship God) to the whole of our lives. How does what we pray one day affect where we spend our time and financial resources on another day? How does praying for, about, and with women affect how we vote and whom we serve? God's loving call in Deuteronomy 6:5, "You shall love the Lord your God with all your heart, all your soul, and all your strength," commands us to integrate our faith into every aspect of our lives, which includes bearing witness to the good, necessary, and powerful work of justice-seeking, beauty-creating, love-making women in the world today.

Jael, a survivor of attempted sexual assault, is like many women today who are survivors of sexual violence and who do not have the resources to seek justice and healing. The **National Sexual Violence Resource Center (NSVRC)** is the leading nonprofit in providing information and tools to prevent and respond to sexual violence. The NSVRC translates research and trends into best practices that help individuals, communities, and service providers achieve real and lasting change. The center also works with the media to promote informed reporting. Every April, NSVRC leads **Sexual Assault Awareness Month (SAAM)**, a campaign to educate and engage the public in addressing this widespread issue.[36]

Learn more about this organization. Continue to support groups in your own communities that promote education, advocacy, and resources about sexual violence in order to end it altogether. Connect. Learn. Give. Grow.

---

[36] McKeever-Burgett, Claire, *Public Witness Woman-Led Nonprofits, https://www.clairemckeeverburgett.com/public-witness, accessed July 10, 2025.*

Chapter Fourteen

Zohara

Protector | Judges 9:50–55

Zohara (name): of Hebrew origin meaning "radiance," "brilliance," or "light"

* * *

Then Abimelech went to Thebez and encamped against Thebez and took it. But there was a strong tower within the city, and all the men and women and all the lords of the city fled to it and shut themselves in, and they went to the roof of the tower. Abimelech came to the tower and fought against it and came near to the entrance of the tower to burn it with fire. But a certain woman threw an upper millstone on Abimelech's head and crushed his skull. 54 Immediately he called to the young man who carried his armor and said to him, "Draw your sword and kill me, so people will not say about me, 'A woman killed him.'" So the young man thrust him through, and he died. When the Israelites saw that Abimelech was dead, they all went home.

—Judges 9:50–55

* * *

ZOHARA'S STORY

Tell me: What would you do if everyone you loved were trapped in a tower, about to be burned to death? Your children, your spouse, your mother, your father, your sister, your brother, your best friend, along with all their children, spouses, mothers and fathers, siblings, and friends?

Would you try to escape? Negotiate? Surrender? Would you let the flames consume you, the screams of your loved ones the last thing you hear before you die?

Tell me. Would you not try to do *something*?

* * *

Having already run from the soldiers trying to kill us, we took shelter in the city's central tower, which contained a gristmill and was the primary source of our food. There was nowhere else to run and nothing else to do but fight or die.

I heard the scritch scratch of hay up against the tower's base, the soldier's curses, and the flints being struck against one another.

This meant only one thing: fire.

Small family groups huddled together, trying to keep warm and afraid to look one another in the eye lest we see in our loved ones' faces what we knew to be true: that the end was near.

I'd given birth to seven children and knew what it was like to come face-to-face with death; so it's not that I wasn't afraid, it's that I knew how to be afraid and not let it paralyze me. When giving birth, freezing is the last thing you want. Movement is your best friend.

Abimelech, the king trying to kill us to conquer our well-positioned and fertile land, stood below the tower laughing, mocking us and our efforts to survive his terror.

This will not be the end, I said, rocking back and forth. *This will not be the last thing we hear.*

* * *

I grab the smallest millstone I can find and begin dragging it across the tower's floor.

People look at me as if I have flames coming out of my head. Maybe I do. A few women and a couple of men rise to help me.

Once we get the millstone to the edge of the tower's wall, we hoist it onto a ledge, allowing it to rest before its long, strategic fall.

What's your plan? they whisper.

Abimelech is circling the tower as his soldiers build up enough hay to start a fire that will consume us. The next time he comes around, I'm going to drop the millstone on top of him.

Their eyes widen. A few heads shake. No one objects.

So, I wait. I can hear him coming by the tenor of his whistle. As if he is celebrating the demise of an entire people. As if what he is doing is no big deal, something to get done before going home.

Meanwhile, my parents and in-laws, my children and their spouses and their children—my grandchildren—hold on for dear life. They are forced to tremble and endure this absurd trauma for no good reason other than Abimelech's need to seek revenge on his brother.

Men and their goddamn wars. When will they learn that violence has never solved a damn thing?

Yet here I am, about to kill a man. One life or hundreds? The choice is clear.

Abimelech stops just below me to relieve himself. A convenient twist of plot. It gives me more time to muster every muscle and adrenaline boost in my body to push the millstone off the ledge.

Squatting like I did in labor, I position my shoulders under the millstone. My people gather around me.

"Count to three," I instruct.

One. They whisper.

I squat lower, readying myself to push.

Two. They exhale.

The millstone cuts into my shoulders. They start to bleed.

Three!

Every muscle and pound of my body digs into the heels of my feet as I push down and then up. I wail as the millstone slides off my back and down the tower's wall.

I hear his whistle, then a thump, then nothing.

Slowly, I peer over the edge and see Abimelech lying on the ground, the millstone pinning his body so that he cannot move.

Abimelech's arms bearer rushes to his side, and though I am too high up to hear what he says, I can see the king point at me with a weak arm before it falls to the ground.

The arms bearer then takes Abimelech's sword and stabs him in the heart, putting him out of his misery.

For a few moments I sit, stunned. Sweat dripping down my face, blood on my shoulders from the heavy imprint of the stone. I fear they will still come for us.

We wait. But no one comes. The soldiers march back to their camp and leave us alone. Slowly, we begin to move. We breathe, smile, and exhale. Then, we embrace and celebrate. We make our way down the tower stairs to ground level. We go home.

* * *

Many weeks later, I received news that Abimelech begged his arms bearer to kill him with his own sword, not to make him suffer less, but so that it wouldn't be said, "Abimelech died at the hands of a woman."

My husband shared this news with me after returning from our neighbor city, Shechem. Apparently, Abimelech's death and our survival was all anyone was talking about throughout the valley.

"It's funny, eh?" my husband said as he removed his sandals, dipping his feet in the washbasin before stepping inside.

"What?" I questioned.

"That the very thing Abimelech didn't want—to be remembered as the king who was killed by a woman—is the very thing everyone is talking about."

"Do they know it was me? I mean, the people who aren't from Thebez?"

"Nah. Nah. They're not concerned with your name. All I heard was 'The Woman of Thebez' spoken like a luscious scandal they couldn't wait to hear more about."

Handing him a towel, I said, "Okay, then. Dinner will be ready in a few minutes. I'm glad you're back."

Later that night as I lay on the hillside staring at the sky, the moon the size of a small fingernail, I told a soft-bosomed, wide-hipped God that I was okay with whatever She needed to do with me, both on earth and beyond.

I know I committed murder, I whispered. *And I wish I were sorry about it, but I'm not.*

Though I didn't hear Her voice audibly, I heard something that sounded like love as a cool breeze swept across my face, signaling a change of season.

The next day in our women's circle, we discussed life and death, good and evil, many of the topics present in the stories passed down about our faith. My mother-in-law, of all women, brought up Gan Eden.

Remember, she said, *Gan Eden is a place of sunshine where all people of all nations will sit and eat together. I think this means that even the most rotten among us will be there because it'll be the kind of place and the kind of table that makes it so.*

Subtly, she reached over and grabbed my hand and gave it a squeeze.

* * *

As we walked back home after the circle, I pulled her aside and asked, "What did you mean by what you said? Do you think I'm rotten because of what I did?"

"Oh honey, no," she said with a sigh. "I was speaking of Abimelech. I like to think Gan Eden will welcome him, too. You? You just did what all the rest of us wanted to do but feared we couldn't. Listen, honey, you don't have to repent for the rest of your life. Lay it down. Let it go. Give yourself a break."

I nodded my acceptance, and I pondered her words in my heart—all easier said than done, though I promised myself right then and there that I would try.

I don't love what I did, but I *do* love who and what it saved.

* * *

Tell me: What would you have done? Back against the wall, loved ones at risk, death so near you could smell it?

I pray you never have to know.

A LITURGY FOR NIGHT PRAYER

OPENING

If you are gathered with others, position yourselves in a circle with enough room to lie on the floor. Invite participants to bring yoga mats and/or blankets for tonight's ritual. If you are alone, find a yoga mat or blanket, place it on the floor, and lie down. Weather permitting, you can also lie down outside in a meadow or field. Either way, anyway, connecting your whole body with the earth, as well as inviting yourself to rest, is essential for the practice of this liturgy. If the conditions allow, light a candle as a sign of connection to the circle of women and the soft-bosomed, wide-hipped God who loves all of us as you pray.

Opening Prayer of Confession

Holy Mother God, we confess before you all the wrongdoing we know to confess, and we admit there's so much we do not know that we lay down before you, too. We trust you to hold it, weave it, spin it, refine it into something new. We do not know much, but we know your love will make it so. Amen.

Psalm 32

Blessed are the women who
think they need to be forgiven,
who walk around feeling guilty and afraid.
The Holy One gives you what you need, when you need it.
Blessed are the women who
think their bodies are sinful and bad
and who deceive their desires
for pleasure and love because of it.

The Holy One gives you abundant permission to please and be pleased, to love and be loved.

Keep silent no more! Tell the Holy One everything.

She is ready to listen. She is always holding.

She is for-giving you whatever it is you need.

If you will only ask. If you will only speak.

Holy One, we lay down before you everything we fear, everything we know, everything we don't know, every terrible thing we've thought, every terrible thing we've done. It's all yours. Help us, we pray! Save us, we pray!

Oh, honey, what even is terrible? What even is wrong? Lay your burdens down. Let them float away in the river, off to somewhere that is no longer your heart. I am here to love.

Blessed are the women who pray to the Holy One,

Whose shoulders relax,

Whose breath returns.

The Holy One breathes new life into us.

Blessed are the women who need a place to hide,

To rest, to be.

The Holy One wraps you in her bosom.

Blessed are the women who are letting go.

The Holy One is with you.

Blessed are the women who are learning to trust a soft-bosomed, wide-hipped God.

The Holy One sees you.

Blessed are the women who find joy again and whose hearts remain open and free.

The Holy One rejoices alongside you.

Amen.

Scripture Reading: Judges 9:50–55

A living, breathing word. **Thanks be to God.**

Silence for prayer and reflection.

Song of Praise

In the Beginning

Claire K. McKeever-Burgett

Contemporary Connection

Take a few moments to listen and watch "Forgiveness" by Patty Griffin and "JUST FOR FUN" by Beyoncé.[37] *Let the melodies, the music, and the words move you toward forgiveness and love. Imagine Zohara singing these songs to herself as she lies in the cool grass in the dark of night, staring at the sky.*

The Prayer of the Women

Holy Mother of sand and sea,

to You all honor and praise.

When we cry out, You hear us.

When we ask for help, You help us.

When we long to be loved, You love us.

May mercy be offered to everyone.

May power and dominion over others cease.

May greed and violence end.

---

[37] McKeever-Burgett, Claire, *Music for Contemporary Connections*, https://www.clairemckeeverburgett.com/*music, accessed July 10, 2025.*

May love live forever.
Birth us into a new world.
Help us make this one beautiful.
Stir us up. Settle us down.
Burn. Simmer. Refine.
When all else shakes, hold us steady.
When everyone else wants to blame,
remind us that in You there is only Love.
Our praise and our prayers are Yours, forever. Amen.

Closing Poem, Forgiveness

Sometimes you must forgive without fanfare or sign,
without the other person knowing.
Forgiveness is for you,
after all.
It's the gift you give yourself
after a long season of letting go.
It's the allowance and the surrender,
the healing and the hope.
No longer about who's right and who's wrong,
it's the mature sibling in the family system who no longer cares who sits where or which of their children Mom and Dad love the most.
The only care in this new world is freedom and joy,
softening and love, gratitude and grace.
Forgiveness is personal, about you and
what your soul, your mind, your body need.
So, open fully to the sun
and bow down before the moon
and let both the dark and the light take you.

REFLECTION QUESTIONS

The following questions are meant to deepen and expand, invite and beckon thoughtful, compassionate, and curious responses to the story and liturgy of Zohara. Whether considering these questions on your own or in a group setting, create space for journaling, collaging, or painting in response. If engaging in group discussion, choose one or two questions, at most, to hold at the center of your sacred circle.

1. What resonates with you about Zohara's story? What feels redemptive? What feels challenging?
2. When reading and praying with Zohara, what sensations do you notice in your body?
3. What does protection mean to you?
4. When have you protected someone who didn't need protecting? When have you failed to protect someone who needed your help?

PUBLIC WITNESS

Because what good are our prayers on Sunday if they make no meaning in our lives on Monday?

Part of our calling as people who claim to follow a God of love, justice, and mercy is to connect what we pray, sing, and hear on Sundays (or the day we set aside to worship God) to the whole of our lives. How does what we pray one day impact where we spend our time and financial resources on another day? How does praying for, about, and with women affect how we vote and who we serve? God's loving call in Deuteronomy 6:5, "You shall love the Lord your God with all your heart, all your soul, and all your strength," commands us to integrate our faith into every aspect of our lives, which includes bearing witness to the good, necessary, and powerful work of justice-seeking, beauty-creating, love-making women in the world today.

Zohara's story of protection in the face of violence leads me to the work of **Women Peace and Security Network Africa**, an organization founded in 2006 under the laws of the Republic of Ghana with the bold vision of creating a violence-free, nondiscriminatory continent that fosters peaceful coexistence, equality, collective ownership, and the full participation of women in decision-making about peace and security. In addition, the **Women's Refugee Commission** works to improve the lives and protect the rights of women, children, youth, and other people who are often overlooked, undervalued, and underserved in humanitarian responses to displacement and crises. I see a woman like Zohara at the helm of each of these modern-day organizations.

Learn more about these organizations. Continue to support groups in your own communities that promote peace, security, and wellbeing for women and people everywhere. Connect. Learn. Give. Grow.[38]

---

[38] McKeever-Burgett, Claire, *Public Witness Woman-Led Nonprofits, https://www.clairemckeeverburgett.com/public-witness, accessed July 10, 2025.*

Chapter Fifteen

Rahab

Deliverer | Joshua 2

Rahab (name): Hebrew meaning "broad," "spacious," or "wide"

* * *

Then Joshua son of Nun sent two men secretly from Shittim as spies, saying, "Go, view the land, especially Jericho." So they went and entered the house of a prostitute whose name was Rahab and spent the night there. The king of Jericho was told, "Some Israelites have come here tonight to search out the land." Then the king of Jericho sent orders to Rahab, "Bring out the men who have come to you, who entered your house, for they have come to search out the whole land." But the woman took the two men and hid them. Then she said, "True, the men came to me, but I did not know where they came from. And when it was time to close the gate at dark, the men went out. Where the men went I do not know. Pursue them quickly, for you can overtake them." She had, however, brought them up to the roof and hidden them with the stalks of flax that she had laid out on the roof. Before they went to sleep, she came up to them on the roof and said to the men, "I know that the Lord has given you the land and that dread of you has fallen on us and that all the inhabitants of the land melt in fear before you. Now then, since I have dealt kindly with you, swear to me by the Lord that you in turn will deal kindly with my family. Give me a sign of good faith that you will spare my father and mother, my brothers and sisters, and all who belong to them and deliver our lives from death." The men said to her, "Our life for yours! If you do not tell this business of ours, then we will deal kindly and faithfully with you when the Lord gives us the land."

—Joshua 2:1–6, 8–9, 12–14

* * *

Author's Note:

In this story, I imagine Rahab as *choosing* her profession as a sex worker instead of being forced into it via enslavement, trafficking, and more, as most girls and women are. My creative decision to have Rahab choose her profession is, I'll admit, a hopeful one, not an ignorant one. The evils and trauma of sex trafficking and sex work, as evidenced in the nonprofits I highlight at the end of the chapter, are rampant and real. Those of us who care about women and girls, justice and love must work to listen and learn from women and their life's circumstances. *What do they want? What do they need?*

My intention with this rendering of Rahab's story is to emphasize the autonomy of a young woman who must go her own way and make a life of her own. I also seek to loosen the stigma of sex work, particularly as the judgment often falls on the bodies and beings of women. What of the men who seek women's bodies for their pleasure? I grew up hearing Rahab's story told as one of redemption—a narrative of how God can use *anyone* to fulfill God's plan, as if Rahab were a tool that God picked up off the ground to use for yardwork. Now, that rendering doesn't sit well with me. Rahab is strong, independent, and unafraid. She is wise, cares deeply about her family, and knows how to save an entire people. If anything, Rahab is the redeemer in this story, and God is her accomplice.

RAHAB'S STORY

Mama screamed the day I left. First, it was a yell. Then, it morphed into a wail. I could almost hear the pieces of her heart breaking apart, shattered on the floor of our simple home. I almost turned around to help clean them up. I almost stayed.

But I made a promise to myself when I was thirteen and coming of age, a promise that I refused to break. It was a contract between the big city of Jericho and me. I said, out loud, "When you call, I will come."

Of course, Jericho had been calling me since I could remember my fat baby legs toddling on the ground. Our small village, located on the outskirts of town, felt suffocating and small even then.

Mama told me stories of the princess who found the baby Moses in the water, of the gold of her palace, of the dark lines framing her eyes, of her jewels and crown. I was mesmerized by the image of her—powerful and poised, decorated and at the lead.

"I'm a princess, Mama," I said when I was three.

"You're *my* princess," she said to me in return.

My family didn't have a lot by way of money or possessions, but we made do. As I grew, I became more and more aware that if I stayed, I would be destined for the simple life of bread-and-baby-making, neither of which ever appealed to me. Sure, I loved my nieces and nephews, many of them more like siblings to me, but I wasn't convinced I wanted to have my own.

I was Mama's surprise. She and Daddy thought they were done having kids until I showed up, curious and craving more, more, more. In fact, according to my mama, "more" was my first word. Barely one year old, Mama says I reached toward Jericho and said, "Mo, Mo, Mo" after visiting its trading hub one day.

"We're going home," she said decisively, "Where you and I belong."

* * *

But I belonged somewhere else, where the music blared, and the lights shone, and the women danced, and the men begged, and the money flowed. I was sixteen and knew it all.

"I'm leaving," I said one night at dinner.

"And just where do you think you're going?" Mama asked.

"To Jericho. There's a place I can live with other women," I said.

"The hell you are," Mama gasped.

"Mama, I'm leaving, and you can't stop me." My mouth, soaked with defiance, left the room with the rest of me.

Daddy simply hung his head. Mama, at first enraged, her face red and hot tears forming behind her eyes, soon fell to the floor in despair.

I grabbed my bag, turned toward the city, and walked away.

* * *

We were sex workers, yes. And we were women who wanted to live our lives on our own terms, free from our families' small minds. The culture demanded our bodies for its pleasure, so we turned its demands into a lucrative business.

It wasn't all sex. We also served food and drink. We offered shows, dancing and singing under the canopy of the night sky. People, not just men, came from near and far to join us—those who blurred the lines of gender. Men who dressed as women; women who dressed as men. Our house, known among the locals as the "Pink Pony Club," became a haven for those who didn't fit into the limitations of cultural convention. It was a safe house for those who needed more space than the world could give them. I was first in line.

I'd always been good with money, so I ended up running the place, taking care of girls thrown to the streets because their moms or dads found them in positions that they didn't want them in. And I set the rules. Customers had to pay up front. Stop, when their companion said so. And, if any violence in word or deed was reported to me, they'd have to pay a hefty fine and leave immediately. I was a no-nonsense kind of woman, and I wanted that same attitude and respect for the others in my care.

* * *

Three men in military uniforms sidle up to the bar, looking for a good time. They ask for a pour. I ask, "What brings you here?"

"We're doing some reconnaissance work," one of them says, "And we need a place to stay for the night. Got any rooms and women available?"

"Depends," I say. "How much you got?"

They slap down several gold coins, and I know they mean business.

After pouring them another round, I signal Donatiya and Hurriya to join the men.

"Show them a good time," I say.

Later that evening, Donatiya pulls me aside.

In a nervous whisper she says, "The king is looking for them. They're Israelites. They need to hide."

"I'll handle it," I say.

After the men have plenty of time letting loose, I lead them up to the roof.

"Sleep here, under the flax. When the king's guards come looking for you, I'll make sure they don't find you."

I'm not sure what motivates me to protect them other than the fact that I have a feeling that Jericho is meant to be the Israelites' land in the first place. I am also always rooting for the underdog, and, in this case, Israel, on the move and without a place to call home, definitely fit the bill.

When the king's guards show up, I lie saying that though we did have a couple of visitors that met their description, they left town hours earlier. The king's guards buy my lie and leave.

Before drifting off to sleep, I climb the stairs to the rooftop to report to the men what had happened.

"I know this land is the Lord's," I confess. "And I know I'm the one who will help you claim it. Because of my kindness and loyalty to you, though, I ask of you one thing: please, when you come to take Jericho, spare the Pink Pony Club, our families, and all who belong to us."

They look at one another and nod.

"Because of your help, we will spare you and yours," they say. "However, you must tie red cloths together, make a rope, and hang it outside your window as a sign of your trust in the God of Israel. Gather up your loved ones. Tell the others to do so, as well. We will return with the force of God."

"May it ever be so," I say, offering a benediction as they climb out of my window and over the wall in the pre-dawn hours.

As soon as they leave, I quickly begin to organize us. Instructing some to be collectors of our families and others to remain in the club and act as though everything is normal, I move with humble haste. We don't have much time.

* * *

I hear my father's voice first. Turning, I see him, flanked by my brothers, their wives, and a horde of children.

He smiles. "So, this is where you've been all this time?"

"Yes, Daddy. This is where I've been. I know it's not what you imagined for me, but it's made me wealthy, happy, and free."

He smiles, a man of very few words.

"Where's Mama?" I inquire, turning my head and standing on my toes looking for her.

"She wouldn't come," he says, his voice full of sadness and regret.

"Mercy," I sigh. "Still stubborn and angry?"

"Still heartbroken and afraid," he says in return.

I know that my only hope of saving my mama is if I go get her myself.

* * *

Walking briskly to our village outside Jericho's city center, it was the first time I had trod that path in more than ten years.

I found Mama pulling weeds in the back garden, tears streaming down her face, sweat mixing with the dirt, making mud.

"Mama," I said, her back to me.

She lifted her head at the sound of my voice.

"Please, Mama, come with me. If you don't, you will die."

"I died a long time ago," she said without turning to me.

"Mama," I cried again, "I love you. I've always loved you. I'm sorry I broke your heart, but we can work it out and find a way to live together again. I have money and a house and food and the promise of protection from the Israelites who are marching, as we speak, toward Jericho."

Mama turned toward me, our eyes meeting for the first time in what felt like forever.

"What have you done?" She spit the words toward me.

"I don't know what you mean," I stammered.

"I'll tell you," she continued. "You sacrificed your family a long time ago when you left. There's no saving me now."

This time, the screams come from inside of me, the shattered pieces of my heart on the ground.

"Don't do this," I whispered.

"It's already done," she said.

* * *

I cry the entire way back to the city. When I arrive, it is dark, typically the time our business picks up for the night. We place a "Closed for Private Event" sign on the door, board the windows, and make our way to the top floor. To create the crimson rope, we each tear a piece of fabric from our robes and headdresses. If they aren't already blood-red, we dip them in a vat of wine to ensure their stain matches the others.

We are a line of misfits and madams, sex workers and singers, gathered with our families (or, at least, with the ones who agreed to come), tying pieces of fabric together to save our lives. If I wasn't so sick with grief after leaving my mama, I might be able to appreciate the moment. Instead, I stare at my daddy and simply shake my head, knotting and tying, knotting and tying until the rope is long enough to reach the ground and wide enough to be seen from afar.

Throwing the rope out the window, we anchor it to the vat of wine in which we stained some of its pieces. Then, we hold on to one another and wait.

* * *

After the Israelites' siege, and after the King of Jericho surrendered, after prisoners were taken captive and the lands surrounding the city center were destroyed, we slowly but surely got back to business as usual. I ensured that Daddy, my brothers, and their families had places to live. I even took a husband, Salmon, and gave birth to a son, Boaz.

We never heard what happened to Mama. I assume she died, one way or another, when the siege took place. Perhaps I married and became a mother because of her. Perhaps I did it out of guilt and sadness, still trying to plead with her, still desperately trying to show her that I could be both a businesswoman *and* a wife, that I could be both a sex worker *and* a mother. Perhaps I married and mothered to appease my own broken heart, to assuage some of my own guilt and grief. Perhaps I did it for all these reasons and more.

Before Daddy died, he looked me in the eye and said, "You delivered us, my daughter. You delivered her, too, even though it may not seem like it. I love you, and she loved you, too."

I wept for days after he died.

***

For years after the invasion of Jericho, the Pink Pony Club continued to shine its lights in the dead of the night, serving up pleasure and making soft beds for people's pain. If its walls could speak, they would tell of sorrow and joy, confusion and ecstasy, mystery and mayhem, freedom and captivity. If its walls could speak, they would tell what any walls would say: that human beings lived and loved here, and that a woman, fierce and fragile, made it so.

***

One of the meanings of my name, Rahab, is "a spacious place," and I like to think my spaciousness is the most accurate thing about me, along with my desire to make life a little more spacious for others. I made space for myself when I was sixteen. I made space for the women and people who lived with me at the Pink Pony Club. I made space for the Israelites to conquer Jericho. I made space for my family and for others' families when they needed refuge and sanctuary. I made space for my husband. I made space for our child.

And, perhaps, today, I will make space for you, as well—to think differently about those who dance the night away. To embrace those who do not fit into society's cultural expectations. To release judgment and fear. To follow your own heart. To love.

As for me, I'm gonna keep on dancing at the Pink Pony Club,[39] spacious, fierce, free.

---

[39] A line from Chappell Roan's song, "Pink Pony Club."

LITURGY FOR NIGHT PRAYER

If you are gathered with others, position yourselves in a circle. Place a lit candle (or disco ball, if you have one!) in the center. If possible, invite participants to bring scraps of red fabric with them. If you are alone, light a candle and have a few scraps of red fabric with you as signs of connection to the circle of women who join you, even here, even now, as you pray.

Opening Prayer of Light

You, Mother God, are our light on dark nights,

and our shade tree on bright days.

You shine in us and through us for all to see.

You are a lamp that guides us to spaciousness and peace.

You are a flame that warms us and keeps us safe.

We gather in the beauty of your light. We rest in the comfort of your darkness.

Amen.

Prayer of Confession and Accountability

For the ways we've made spaces too small for Your beloved children, **forgive us.**

For the ways we've broken one another's hearts, even when we intended the exact opposite, **heal us.**

For the ways we've broken Your heart, Mother God, **have mercy on us.**

That in forgiveness, healing, and mercy, we may find lit up places to dance in the joy of our deliverance for the sake of Love, Freedom, and Joy for all, with all, and in all. Amen.

Psalm 130

With our hearts broken into pieces on the floor,

cries billow up and out of us,

turning into wails.

Hear us, Mother God,

as we stomp our feet

and sway our hips.

All we really want is mercy,
acceptance,
a spacious place to live.
In your arms You enfold us,
offering forgiveness and love
so that when the time comes, we
can tie scraps of fabric together
to be rescued and saved and to
save and rescue.
So, we wait with hope for You, Mother God,
with heart, mind, soul, and body.
Throughout the night, we wait.
Your love rises with the sun.
Your redemption wakes us up.
Your joy is our salvation. **Amen.**

Scripture Reading: Joshua 2

A living, breathing word. **Thanks be to God.**

Silence for prayer and reflection.

Song of Praise

In the Beginning

Claire K. McKeever-Burgett

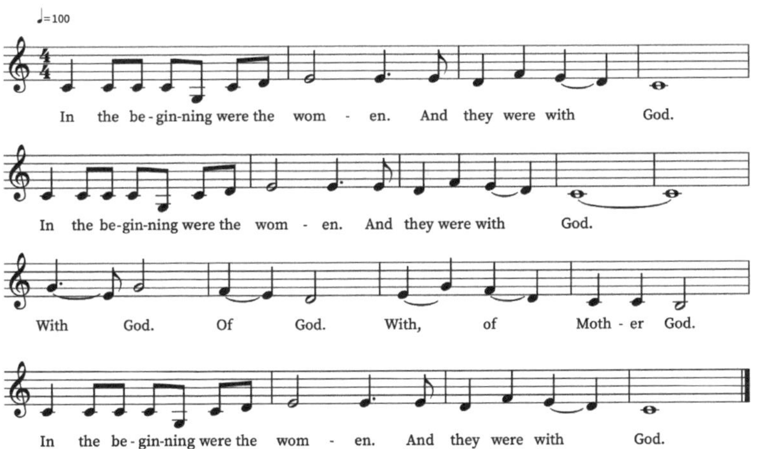

Contemporary Connection

Take a few moments to watch and listen to "Pink Pony Club" by Chappell Roan,[40] *the song which inspired my version of Rahab's story. Let yourself sing and dance, imagining Rahab and her loved ones doing the same. Invite this song to join you in your prayerful, worshipful, songful life.*

The Prayer of the Women

Holy Mother of sand and sea,
to You all honor and praise.
When we cry out, You hear us.
When we ask for help, You help us.
When we long to be loved, You love us.
May mercy be offered to everyone.
May power and dominion over others cease.
May greed and violence end.
May love live forever.
Birth us into a new world.
Help us make this one beautiful.
Stir us up. Settle us down.
Burn. Simmer. Refine.
When all else shakes, hold us steady.
When everyone else wants to blame,
remind us that in You there is only Love.
Our praise and our prayers are Yours, forever. Amen.

REFLECTION QUESTIONS

The following questions are meant to deepen and expand, invite and beckon thoughtful, compassionate, and curious responses to the story and liturgy of Rahab. Whether considering these questions on your

---

[40] McKeever-Burgett, Claire, *Music for Contemporary Connections,* https://www.clairemckeeverburgett.com/*music, accessed July 10, 2025.*

own or in a group setting, create space for journaling, collaging, or painting in response. If engaging in group discussion, choose one or two questions, at most, to hold at the center of your sacred circle.

1. What resonates with you about Rahab's story? What feels redemptive? What feels challenging?
2. When reading and praying with Rahab, what sensations do you notice in your body?
3. What does deliverance and spaciousness mean to you?
4. If you were to own a club, which became a haven for all kinds of people, what would you name it and why?

PUBLIC WITNESS

Because what good are our prayers on Sunday if they make no meaning in our lives on Monday?

Part of our calling as people who claim to follow a God of love, justice, and mercy is to connect what we pray, sing, and hear on Sundays (or the day we set aside to worship God) to the whole of our lives. How does what we pray one day affect where we spend our time and financial resources on another day? How does praying for, about, and with women affect how we vote and whom we serve? God's loving call in Deuteronomy 6:5, "You shall love the Lord your God with all your heart, all your soul, and all your strength," commands us to integrate our faith into every aspect of our lives, which includes bearing witness to the good, necessary, and powerful work of justice-seeking, beauty-creating, love-making women in the world today.

Though I imagine Rahab's club and life to be a safe place for the outcast women and people of Jericho, this is definitely *not* the case for most girls and women who've been sex trafficked throughout time and who are still to this day trafficked without their consent. **Lovely Village**, a nonprofit founded by my friends, Emily and Brett Mills, is a healing community for survivors of sexual trauma. Through building trauma-informed communities, justice enterprises that create boutique-quality, ethically sourced and socially responsible products made by survivors, and innovative artistic programs that seek to inspire people to meaningful action, **Lovely Village** creates safe housing, living-wage jobs, and sustainable long-term livelihoods for survivors of sexual trauma.

POETIC is a nonprofit organization in Dallas, Texas that equips girls who have experienced child mistreatment, commercial sexual exploitation, and sex trafficking to find their voices, reclaim their narratives, and move forward with their lives. The inspiring vision of POETIC rejects the notion that youth can be bought and sold and imagines a world in which all children are equally valued and loved.

Learn more about these organizations. Continue to support groups in your own communities that support survivors of sexual trauma and human trafficking, create safe, sustainable communities, and empower girls to reclaim their voices, tell their stories, and persist in love. Connect. Learn. Give. Grow.[41]

[41] McKeever-Burgett, Claire, *Public Witness Woman-Led Nonprofits, https://www.clairemckeeverburgett.com/public-witness, accessed July 10, 2025.*

Chapter Sixteen

Imma

Wisdom Warrior | 2 Samuel 20: 14–22

Imma (name): of Hebrew origin meaning "mother"

* * *

*Sheba passed through all the tribes of Israel to Abel of Beth-maacah, and
all the Bichrites assembled and followed him inside. Joab's forces came
and besieged him in Abel of Beth-maacah; they threw up a siege ramp
against the city, and it stood against the rampart. Joab's forces were
battering the wall to break it down. Then a wise woman called from the
city, "Listen! Listen! Tell Joab, 'Come here, I want to speak to you.'" 17
He came near her, and the woman said, "Are you Joab?" He answered,
"I am." Then she said to him, "Listen to the words of your servant."
He answered, "I am listening." Then she said, "They used to say in the
old days, 'Let them inquire at Abel,' and so they would settle a matter.
I am one of those who are peaceable and faithful in Israel; you seek to
destroy a city that is a mother in Israel; why will you swallow up the
heritage of the Lord?" Joab answered, "Far be it from me, far be it, that
I should swallow up or destroy! That is not the case! But a man of the
hill country of Ephraim called Sheba son of Bichri has lifted up his hand
against King David; give him up alone, and I will withdraw from the
city." The woman said to Joab, "His head shall be thrown over the wall
to you." Then the woman went to all the people with her wise plan. And
they cut off the head of Sheba son of Bichri and threw it out to Joab. So
he blew the trumpet, and they dispersed from the city, and all went to
their homes, while Joab returned to Jerusalem to the king.*

—2 Samuel 20:14–22

* * *

IMMA'S STORY

My head jerks upward as the ground shakes. Instinctively, I know that an army marches toward us. Quickly, I find my children, instructing them to hide.

"How long, Mama?" one of them asks, groggy and still half asleep.

"Until I return," I say.

My oldest, Rachel, catches my eyes. For a few moments we hold each other's gaze. Without saying a word, she knows what she needs to do.

"Come along," Rachel says, gently ushering her siblings into the bunker. "We'll be safe here. Do as Mother says."

"I love you, all," I say to them as I leave, heading straight for the city wall.

* * *

Years ago, when I was only four years old, my great aunt was a woman to whom many have turned in times of distress. She would meet people on the streets, by the shoreside, at the market. People from far and near sought her out. Her favorite place to receive people was under a sycamore tree.

I was often playing with my cousins nearby, throwing rocks, using sticks as swords, pretending to be warriors fighting off the enemy.

My great aunt approached us one day as we moved the sticks back and forth in our hands, striking them against each other.

"You know true warriors fight with their words, not their swords," she said.

It felt as if she were throwing the words away, as they were directed at no one in particular.

We paused our war game for a few moments as she passed and reached for the water jug. I watched her pour the water down her throat, letting it drip down her chin and onto her neck, shoulders, and chest, almost as if she were drinking and bathing at the same time. With a pronounced release of the jug back onto the ground, she slung her forearm across her face, wiping off the excess water. Then, she simply turned around and walked back to her place under a sycamore tree.

As soon as she resumed her position, we went back to playing. We kicked and punched the air, mimicking what we saw our fathers and uncles do as they prepared for war. Though I was a girl, I got away with playing war because I was so young, and Mama and my aunties needed a break from my constant neediness. I didn't know any women who were warriors, though I'd heard tales whispered by the firelight late in the night.

When I was supposed to be sleeping, I'd crawl out of bed and listen to my grandmother and aunties speak and sing of warrior women who protected and loved, led and told the truth.

She breathes fire, they would say of one woman.

Her songs put people in a trance, they'd say of another.

She flies. She dances. She shoots. She soars.

My eyes would grow large, and my mouth would fall agape. So amazed and inspired was I by the possibility of women who fought. Could it be that we breathed the same air, trod the same ground, lived on the same earth?

It was almost too much for my young heart to hold.

* * *

Because I know the city wall like I know the back of my hand, I walk straight toward the place where I can get a message to the king. All around me, chaos ensues. People run frantically in the streets, desperate to find their loved ones before the attack begins. I'm not the only one who feels the earth shake and knows what it means.

Children cry. Mothers wail. Men yell. Soldiers arm themselves.

I continue walking toward the wall.

* * *

When I turned thirteen, instead of being married off to a man, my mother and grandmother came to me with a proposition.

"Learn from your great aunt," they said. "You can get married in a few years. For now, sit at her feet under the sycamore tree, and listen."

A smile spread across my round face. "Really?" I asked.

"Really," they said.

Squealing with glee, I hugged both, crying, "Thank you, thank you, thank you, thank you."

The next day, I joined my great aunt in her usual spot, expecting to receive a warm welcome. Instead, I was met with a gruff grunt and a, "Sit there and be quiet."

One by one they came.

How do my sister and I reconcile our differences? What is the meaning of life? Why does he have more goats than me when I'm the one who paid for them?

No problem was too small for her to address, no person too insignificant. She treated everyone the same, answering them with questions instead of statements, offering riddles to make them think. At every turn, she would say things like, "You ask me what you already know" and "What does it mean to love?" and "True wisdom grows within, but you must become quiet in order to hear it."

Day after day, I sat at her feet, listened, and eventually began to learn that what she had said to me when I was four was true. True warriors fight with their words, not with their swords.

* * *

I arrive at the city wall, where an opening to the outside world exists. The architects of the wall placed small openings at strategic points for messages and wagers to be passed back and forth. Small windows. I wonder whether the builders realized how the light would shine through them creating bright slivers on the ground.

The earth continues to shake as the stomps and chants of the opposing army grow louder. I hear the thud of stone upon the dirt. Through the small hole in the wall I see their army is building a siege ramp of debris and timber. They will breach our city wall in no time.

* * *

Though I sat at my great aunt's feet listening and learning, I still longed for the battlefield. I wanted to fight with a sword and my hands. I wanted to be one of the women warriors of whom people spoke with awe and wonder around the fire.

Therefore, every morning and evening, I'd make my way to the woods and train.

Jab, cross, hook.

I punched the air, right foot forward, standing at the ready.

Front push, roundhouse, spinning back kick.

I sliced the air with my legs, fists in front of my face.

Again and again, I'd kick the air and punch the imaginary person in front of me, training my body for a battle I would never fight.

Though I remained unmarried for a few years, as Mother and Grandmother promised, at the age of seventeen my parents married me to Ahad. Soon thereafter, I became pregnant with Rachel. A year later, I pushed Jonas out of me, and then came the twins, Ezra and Eli. Finally, I gave birth to another girl, Johanna. Feeding and nurturing children took precedence over training for imaginary battles. In those early years of raising young ones, I didn't even have time to sit with my great aunt under the sycamore tree.

Mama, I'm hungry. Mama, I'm thirsty. Mama, Mama, Mama.

My children's voices soothed and grated all at once. They were all I could hear.

* * *

I hear the voices of children now as I hoist myself upon a ledge, finding leverage and balance in front of the small opening in the wall.

Fitting my mouth in the opening, I begin to speak.

"Listen! Listen! Tell Joab I want to speak to him!"

At first, the soldiers ignore me. Or perhaps they can't hear me above the ramp-building din.

I yell again, "Listen! Listen! Tell Joab I want to speak to him!"

Finally, one of the men looks up, signaling to the others to stop their labor.

"Listen! Listen!" I yell again. "Tell Joab I want to speak to him!"

Turning toward me, the soldier, bemused and grinning, walks to the opening in the wall where I peer outward.

"What is it you want?" he spits at me.

"Joab. Your king. I want to speak with him!" I reply.

To my surprise, he turns back toward the men, yelling, "She wants to speak to the king. So let's get her the king!"

A raucous laughter erupts among them. Apparently, I'm a joke.

Still, they send for the king. A welcome break from their building, they sit back to watch the show.

King Joab approaches the opening in the wall. I'm surprised to see how small he is. Short, squat, and soft, he doesn't fit my visions of what a king should look like. He wears a crown and thick armor. He is flanked by guards and walks as though he is ten feet tall.

* * *

Only in recent years have I had the energy, time, and space to return to my wisdom seeking and sharing. My great aunt died when my youngest child turned five, leaving a vacancy for the role of wise woman in our town.

She took her last breath while leaning against the sycamore tree. We found her, dead and smiling.

At my great aunt's burial, Grandmother turned to me and said, "It's your time now."

Without saying a word in return, I knew what she meant. An informal passing of the mantle, the role of wise woman was now mine for the taking.

Late one night, restless and unable to sleep, I turned to Ahad.

"I want to be a warrior," I whispered.

"Then be one," he whispered back, before turning over and settling quickly into a snore-filled sleep.

The next morning, instead of making my way to the woods to kick the air and punch the trees, I made my way to my late aunt's tree. My children played in the open space near me, their giggles a welcome background chorus for the day.

People came from far and near, seeking wisdom.

I heard myself saying to them, "What does your heart want?" and "What does freedom mean to you?" and "Drink some water and take some deep breaths before doing anything."

Out of the corner of my eye, I saw Rachel, Jonas, Ezra, Eli, and Johanna playing war. Three against two, they used sticks and fists to punch the air and jab their pretend enemies.

Remembering what my great aunt said to me all those years ago, I smiled, breathed, and walked toward the jug of water.

"You know that true warriors fight with their words, not their swords," I said to my kids before picking up the jug.

They stopped their playing and watched me pour the water down my throat before I walked back to my place under the tree. Once I'd resumed my position, they began playing again.

* * *

"Are you Joab?" I ask.

"I am," he replies.

"Please listen to me," I beg.

"I will listen," he says in return.

"For years," I begin, "People have come from near and far to seek wisdom here in the city of Abel. My great aunt sat under a sycamore tree and settled matters, one after another. I now inhabit her role, offering the same. I am one of the peaceable and faithful in Israel."

I pause to take a breath. The king's face twitches. "Keep talking!" he commands.

"You seek to destroy a city that is a mother in Israel. We have nurtured and led people for years. Our destruction will mean not only the demise of a city, but of a city that houses the wisdom heritage of the Lord. Is this what you want?" I implore.

Joab speaks immediately.

"Far be it from me that I would eat and swallow up the city of Abel! But there is a man here named Sheba, son of Bichri, who has defied King David. If you give him up alone, I will withdraw my troops from your city today."

"Very well, then," I say. "You will have Sheba's head thrown to you over the wall this very day."

* * *

I run to the sycamore tree, and the people follow. As the crowd gathers, I announce the plan that will save us.

"We must find Sheba, cut off his head, and throw it over the wall!"

"I know where Sheba is hiding," a woman yells from the crowd.

"Take us to him!" another one yells.

A collective roar waves through the crowd as they follow the woman to where Sheba hides. I remain at the sycamore tree, awaiting Sheba's head. I will be the one to throw it over the wall, delivering it to King Joab.

It doesn't take long for them to return with the bloody head of Sheba. It is heavier than I expect. It smells of blood and bile. Regardless of the gruesome task, all I can think about is returning to my children, where they hide in the bunker.

So, I walk toward the wall. This time, I hear no screams or frantic movements from the people. They are quiet and still, watching me as I place one foot in front of the other.

Arriving at the wall, I heave Sheba's head over my shoulder and with every muscle in my body, hurl it over the wall's edge.

With a thud, his head lands. For a moment, there's nothing but silence, save a crow cawing in the distance. Then, like a royal welcome on a wedding day, we hear the trumpet sound, announcing the army's retreat from our city.

As the last note fades, the people of Abel break into cheers and laughter, yelling with glee. They clap and stomp, dance and celebrate. They pass jugs of wine from person to person. They break and share loaves of bread.

* * *

I make my way back to my children. Rachel has her arms around the twins and Johanna. Jonas sits, fidgeting with a stick.

"Hello, my loves," I say to them.

They look up with big, expectant eyes.

"Is it over, Mama?" they ask.

"Yes, it is over," I reply.

Opening my arms wide, I welcome them back into the fold of their mama's skin. I hold them for as long as they'll let me; I may never let go.

Later that night, Rachel comes to me, unable to sleep.

"Mama, are you a warrior or a wise woman?" she asks.

I consider her question, the two lines between my eyebrows crinkling as I think. She has the insight of her great aunt and the curiosity of her mother.

"I am both," I finally say.

Rachel nods her head convincingly. She knows. She is wise beyond her years.

* * *

I make my way to the sycamore tree early the next morning before the sun rises. It is still dark, and I can barely see an inch or two in front of me, but I know the way to the tree with my eyes closed.

I can't stop thinking about yesterday's events. How the muscles I grew when training in the woods and lifting young children onto my hips helped me heave Sheba's head over the wall. How the depth I cultivated by sitting and listening to my great aunt helped me broker peace with a king. How, in the end, it was both words and swords that kept the people of Abel alive.

Looking to the east, I see the sun begin to peak above the horizon. For a moment, I see my great aunt standing there, flanked by other women. For a moment, they smile at me, their smiles a blessing.

* * *

The city of Abel, a mother in Israel, continues to thrive and live for a very long time. Rachel, eventually, takes my place under the sycamore tree. I, eventually, grow old and die.

Time and its passing offer both comfort and worry, as they always have and always will. Women offer both wisdom and arms, as they always have and always will. Women fight with their words and with their swords to protect the cities and the people they love.

On and on it goes throughout the years. *Is she a warrior or a wise woman? A mother or a mystic?* people ask, the people wonder.

Why can't she be all of these and more?

The question comes from the back of the room in which the people debate a woman's place—*Is it on the battlefield or in the birthing room? Is it at the bedside or in the war room?*

The people turn toward the voice who asked the question and see a young woman, maybe sixteen or seventeen, standing. She is undeterred by their stares.

What did you say? they ask.

Why can't she be all of these and more? the young woman asks again.

A hush falls over the crowd. They've never really thought about it like that before. A woman being multidimensional and complex.

Finally, their leader speaks. *We don't know why not.* They say with honesty to the young woman.

Perhaps, then, we need to ask different questions. The young woman walks to the center of the room. Everyone's eyes follow her as she moves.

What if instead of "Where is a woman's place?" and "Is she this or that?" we ask, "What multitudes does she contain? What power does she embody?"

The people sigh. The young woman remains. No one speaks for a very long time. Then, someone says to the young woman, *What is your name?*

Imma, she says. *I'm named after my great-great-grandmother.*

Ah, Mother, they say, reciting the meaning of her name.

Mother, she says quietly. *And warrior. And wisdom teacher. And mystic, prophet, poet, priest. I contain multitudes*, she says, as she walks away from the people toward a sycamore tree where she sits and rests under its shade, awaiting all who long for wisdom and are willing to let it transform their lives.

I smile from above, witnessing my great-great-granddaughter follow in my footsteps and live in her truth. I smile as I witness women's intricate power on display—mothers, mystics, wise women, and warriors together, with Mother God, loving the world again and again and again and again.

Amen.

A LITURGY FOR EVENING PRAYER

Whether you are gathered with others or alone, consider practicing this liturgy outside, weather permitting, of course. Invite the sun or the moon to serve as your candle/light. If outside is inaccessible, find a place to sit as close and comfortably to the ground or floor as possible. Breathe. Trust that the women and Holy Mother God are with you, here and now, as you worship, pray, and sing.

Opening Witness

May we be faithful companions to ourselves and others in this life.

May we know a love like Imma's love for her city and her children.

May we trust that Mother God will not forsake us.

May we believe that another world is possible.

Amen.

Evening Prayer

We see Your Love, O God, in the ways in which we love one another. Under the moon, in the midday sun, and when there is no light to be found. In every color, every season, every shadow, every tint, every phase, You bind us to one another and to You. Thanks be to God. Amen.

Psalm 25

In Mother God, we trust. She shows us what wisdom looks like.

She goes before us to set up camp and make a way.

Mother God will never let shame have the last word.

She puts shame to rest.

Show us the way to women warriors, who,

with Your strength and wisdom, protect us on the

paths of our lives.

Guide us toward truth-tellers and teach us

words of honesty, Mother God.

For just as Imma held hope like a guiding light,

so we hope for You all day and all night long.

Remember us, Mother God, in your mercy and love.

Relieve the worries of our hearts, free us from our anguish

so that we might come alongside others in steadfastness and love for the rest of our days…and even in the great beyond. Amen.

Scripture Reading: 2 Samuel 20: 14–22

A living Word for a living people. **Thanks be to God.**

A moment of quiet for prayer and reflection.

Prayers of the People

Holy Mother God, we pray to you now, in the spirit of Imma and wise warrior mystic mother women everywhere, asking for your blessing, protection, and love for all people, particularly for those maligned by and caught within systems they didn't create. For new imaginations, close connections, and loving companions, we pray.

Silence

Holy Mother God, our hearts, minds, bodies, and spirits are tired. Like Imma, the loads we carry are heavy. Send us loved ones who make the loads lighter just by being near us. Help all people who listen to Your divine feminine wisdom grow throughout the lands. Give them joy. Give them justice. Give them freedom.

Silence

Holy Mother God, we know how to be wise with our words because of You. Dancing with the face of the deep, befriending chaos, inviting all to join in the acts of creation, You are our friend, and we are grateful. May we join you in your creative work as old ways die and new ones are born.

Silence

For the world at large and for the many worlds that make up our daily lives, we give You thanks and we continuously pray in Your Wise and Holy Name…

Amen.

Song of Praise

In the Beginning

Claire K. McKeever-Burgett

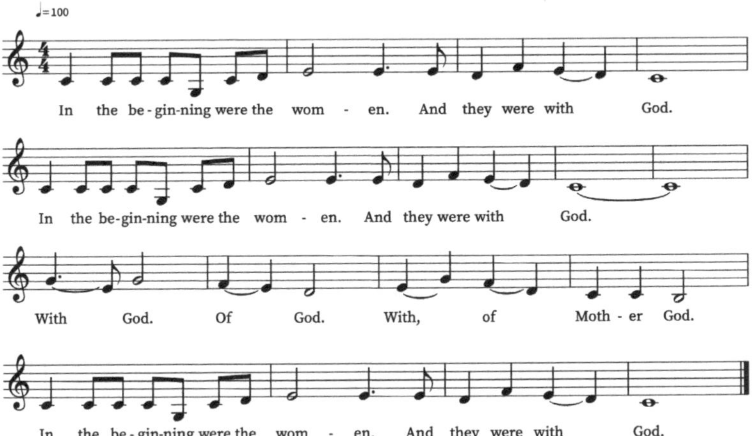

Contemporary Connection

Take a few moments to listen to and watch "For Good" from the musical Wicked, performed by Kristin Chenoweth and Idina Menzel.[42] *As you listen and watch, imagine Imma singing this song with her great aunt, her daughter, Rachel, and others. Consider who has changed you for good. Who has protected and loved you with their actions and their words. Invite this song into your prayerful, worshipful, songful life.*

The Prayer of the Women

Holy Mother of sand and sea,
to You all honor and praise.
When we cry out, You hear us.
When we ask for help, You help us.
When we long to be loved, You love us.
May mercy be offered to everyone.
May power and dominion over others cease.
May greed and violence end.
May love live forever.
Birth us into a new world.
Help us make this one beautiful.
Stir us up. Settle us down.
Burn. Simmer. Refine.
When all else shakes, hold us steady.
When everyone else wants to blame,
remind us that in You there is only Love.
Our praise and our prayers are Yours, forever. Amen.

REFLECTION QUESTIONS

The following questions are meant to deepen and expand, invite and beckon thoughtful, compassionate, and curious responses to the story and liturgy of Imma. Whether considering these questions on

[42] McKeever-Burgett, Claire, *Music for Contemporary Connections,* https://www.clairemckeeverburgett.com/*music, accessed July 10, 2025.*

your own or in a group setting, create space for journaling, collaging, or painting in response. If engaging in group discussion, choose one or two questions, at most, to hold at the center of your sacred circle.

1. What resonates with you about Imma's story? What feels redemptive? What feels challenging?
2. When reading and praying with Imma, Mother God, and the women what sensations do you notice in your body?
3. What does "mother" mean to you? What does protection look like in your life?
4. When have you used both your words and actions to demonstrate love?

PUBLIC WITNESS

Because what good are our prayers on Sunday if they make no meaning in our lives on Monday?

Part of our calling as people who claim to follow a God of love, justice, and mercy is to connect what we pray, sing, and hear on Sundays (or the day we set aside to worship God) to the whole of our lives. How does what we pray one day affect where we spend our time and financial resources on another day? How does praying for, about, and with women affect how we vote and whom we serve? God's loving call in Deuteronomy 6:5, "You shall love the Lord your God with all your heart, all your soul, and all your strength," commands us to integrate our faith into every aspect of our lives, which includes bearing witness to the good, necessary, and powerful work of justice-seeking, beauty-creating, love-making women in the world today.

Though Imma is not actually an immigrant, refugee, domestic worker, or farmworker, she comes close to being at least a few of these when her beloved city is threatened with attack. She is also connected to domestic work as a mother. The **Tennessee Immigrant and Refugee Rights Coalition (TIRRC)**, located in Nashville, TN, organizes both individual immigrants and refugees, as well as organizations and multifaith congregations that serve immigrant and refugee communities to build power, amplify refugee and immigrant voices, and organize communities to advocate for refugee and immigrant rights. The TIRRC is a part of the **National Domestic**

Workers Alliance, which works to win respect, recognition, and labor rights and protections for the nearly 2.5 million nannies, house cleaners, and homecare workers who do the essential work of caring for our loved ones and our homes. Finally, **Farmworker Justice** fights for farmworkers' rights, ensures safe working conditions, promotes access to healthcare, and empowers farmworkers to know their rights and organize to effect change for themselves and others. They also shine a spotlight on the **importance of farmworker women and representation,** as 80 percent of women farmworkers are, to this day, still sexually harassed on the job.

Learn more about these organizations. Continue to support groups in your own communities that promote immigrant, refugee, domestic worker, and farmworker rights. Connect. Learn. Give. Grow.[43]

---

[43] McKeever-Burgett, Claire, *Public Witness Woman-Led Nonprofits, https://www.clairemckeeverburgett.com/public-witness, accessed July 10, 2025.*

Epilogue + Benediction

Imagine the daughter from the prologue. Her mother has now died and left the earth; she is older and a mother herself. In many ways, she is like me—searching for women's stories, voices, names, and imaginations. Perhaps you may also relate to the daughter who longs for a different way of being in the world, a way that centers and celebrates the divine feminine spirit within all of us. She is working, day by day, to leave her children a legacy of love. I imagine the daughter as an ancient woman because it consoles me to think that our ancestors, like us, have been working to unearth and make their stories anew from the very beginning. It's not as if all a sudden I am here as an intersectional feminist storyteller and theologian. No, women like the ones I write about in this book and in both the prologue and epilogue—women like you and women like me—have been paving the way since the beginning of time so that our voices and stories remain and can be made new.

I was a child when my mother first whispered to me that women were there with God in the very beginning. Half asleep, she would wrap her arms around me, snuggling close to keep me warm. She smelled of smoke and sage, and to this very day, when I smell either, I smile.

In the beginning were the women, she would whisper. *And they were with God and they were of God.*

In my sleepy stupor, I would nod, reach for her arm, and pull it tighter around me. It was my security blanket. At the time, if you'd asked me to explain what she meant, I would've said, "I don't know," before running after my brother to play a game of tag.

Now, the vision of women and God, God and women is something I know deep in my bones. It has become my practice, my ritual, my prayer. It has become for me an entire belief system built on the premise that women are not accessories to the story, but the very story themselves. That without them, without *us*, there'd be very little of which to speak, pray, sing, and believe. That without us, the story is incomplete.

So, I set about the work my mother began. Culling through scraps of papyrus, discerning messages carved into stone, listening to aunties and sisters, midwives and mothers recount the drama and mundanity of their lives, I was able to patch together *herstory* instead of history. I heard the names of the women, some of them for the very first time. I sang the songs of the women even when I didn't know the tune.

I now share these names and tales with my daughter *and* with my son. He, too, learns about the blood of birth, the challenges of motherhood, and the desperation to protect those whom you love. He, too, listens to the ancestor's whisper: *In the beginning were the women. And the women were with God, and the women were of God.* And in hearing and learning alongside women, he, too, is transformed.

In all my research and discovery of unearthing women's stories, a common theme kept surfacing: though women found strength and protection in community with one another, their wisdom, spirituality, and love were for everyone. They longed for their sons to be liberated from patriarchy, too, not just their daughters. Thus, to know women's stories is to know that the divine feminine lives within us all; that Mother God is waiting to be awakened and accessed for the sake of love. After all, true liberation sets everybody free.

* * *

The light is bright and warm. Shade trees, with large trunks and deep roots, provide shelter. Music, soft and rhythmic, soothes the well-worn heart. Women stand, dance, sway, and sing *with* God and *of* God as it was in the beginning. Their arms, like God's, open wide so every one of us can crawl into the soft, warm middle, curl up, and rest.

At first, my son and my daughter are hesitant to join us. Their faces ask: *Is this what grandmother was always yammering on about? Is this the thing to which you've dedicated your life?*

I reach my hands toward them, welcoming them into the circle. Reluctantly, they join.

Out of the corner of my eye, I notice each of them holds something in their hands.

What do you have? I ask.

Without speaking, my son opens his palm, revealing two stones. My daughter, then, opens her palm to show dried sage, picked from our garden last week.

For the fire, my son says.

For Grandmother, my daughter says.

I smile, large tears rolling down my face. It's all I can do to mouth the words "thank you" to each of them.

Then, my son begins to strike the stones against one another, and my daughter fans the flame. The women join my daughter in fanning the flames until they grow larger, higher, warmer. Smoke and sage mingle in the air, drift inside my nostrils, and tangle in my hair. For a moment, when I close my eyes, I can see my mother among us. She dances and sings. She is free.

* * *

In the end, the work of justice, mercy, and love gets done because someone whispers in their child's ear the story of women and God, and they continue whispering the truth until it sinks into their bones like it did into mine. They pray the prayers and sing the songs and name the women out loud. They tell the stories. They retell them. They tell them over again.

Yes, the work of justice, mercy, and love gets done because a host of beautiful people care enough to know and witness the women, who are *with* God and *of* God, as it was in the beginning, is now and ever shall be, world without end, amen and amen.

* * *

Go forth, beloveds, listening and learning anew the stories of the women who've always been, are, and forever will be with God and with you. Amen.

APPENDIX

Story as Spiritual Practice

A faithful, usable guide for applying story as spiritual practice in your daily life.

EMBODIMENT

FIRST, get in your body! The work of centering and celebrating women's stories is not for the head alone. We must integrate the fullness of our minds, bodies, and spirits to practice the stories we long to tell.

1. Before reading scripture or telling a story, place both feet on the ground and settle your shoulders away from your ears. Take a few deep breaths, in through your nose, out through your mouth. Rest your hands, palms down, on the tops of your thighs as you breathe.

2. When you're ready to receive whatever Spirit has for you today, turn your palms over, facing upward, and say, "I am here—mind, body, and spirit." Continue to breathe in through your nose and out through your mouth.

3. Then, bring your hands to your heart and your belly. Continue to breathe deeply and allow yourself to feel your heartbeat, the softness of your skin. When you're ready, say, "My heart is open, my belly is beautiful."

4. Now, stand, if you're willing and able. If you need to remain seated, simply follow the arm and hand motions as outlined next while in your chair. Ground both feet into the earth, balancing your weight on both feet. Reach your arms out to the sides and then up to the sky. Let your eyes and head look up. Continuing to breathe deeply and say, "I am here—mind, body, and spirit."

5. Begin to sway back and forth, moving through your arms, your head, your shoulders, your belly, your hips, thighs, and legs. Slowly bring your arms down to your sides.

6. In a standing position (or seated, as needed), begin to shake your arms, releasing any tension you are holding. When you feel ready, settle into a still standing position and bring your hands to your heart and belly once again. Breathe deeply.

7. Nod your head "yes." Shake your head "no." Both are important words to say. Both are important movements to make.

8. Finally, wrap your arms around the middle of your body and squeeze, giving yourself a hug. Say, "All of me is here. All of me is beautiful."

9. Then, release your arms, slowly, and, if standing, find your way back to a seated position.

ENGAGEMENT

NOW that you've invited the integration of mind, body, and spirit, begin engaging with a sacred story. Here's how:

1. **Remember** that scripture is the living word, an ever evolving and developing story to which we bring our whole selves and with which we are in conversation as we live out our own faith with awe, wonder, reverence, and honesty.

2. **Be curious**. Ask questions of the Bible, the story, the liturgy, the hymns, God, anything and everything! Ask, "Where are the women?" Because even if they're not there, they're there. Who gave birth to Moses? Who were Eve's daughters? Who were the concubines of David?

3. **Create Community**. Find communities that invite questions and mystery into their communal worship and practices. Connect with communities that welcome your curiosity and challenges. Spend time with communities that center women and their stories.

4. **Know God's Many Names**. *Shekinah* (divine presence in female form) in the midrashim, *Eloah* (gives birth as a woman) in Deut. 32:18b, *Chokmah* (Woman Wisdom) in Proverbs, *Mother Hen* in Luke 13:34. Knowing the many names for God can help broaden our understanding of who God is, how God works, and whom God loves—everyone.

5. **Begin to retell, name, and reclaim** the stories for yourself and for others. For example, when reading about the mighty King David in the Hebrew Bible, consider: Who are his sisters? What are their names? Whom and what do they love? What's their favorite food? What do they enjoy doing? What drives them crazy? What, if anything, do they think of their brother, David?
6. **Use your God-given imagination and creativity**. Genesis 1:27–28 says, "God created humans in God's image. And God blessed them." From the very beginning, God is a creative God. God makes trees and animals and oceans and light! And then, God makes us like God. Which means that from the beginning we have been given the same playfulness, whimsy, creativity, and imaginative spirit as God. Blessed by God, we are then sent forth to create! To play! To imagine and reimagine! So, instead of keeping your curiosity and wonder tightly bound, loosen them. Let them run free. In their freedom, new stories, worlds, and love are to be found.

Small Group Guide

Given that one of the steps of "Story as Spiritual Practice" is to create and find community, the small group guide offers a structure and rhythm for engaging each chapter of this book with groups. I recommend gathering in circles of no more than eight to ensure group cohesion and connection. Women have been gathering in circles for centuries, so it feels right to follow their lead and do the same.

PRE-GATHERING

1. Of the eight or fewer participants, one person will serve as Convener for each week. Invite each person to sign up for the week that works best for them to serve in this role. Encourage each member of the group to serve as Convener at least once. Because there are sixteen women's stories, each group member will serve as Convener twice.
2. The Weekly Convener is responsible for ensuring that the group knows which story it will be reading for the week, for bringing a candle for the center of the small group circle, and for ensuring that all members have a copy of the book and therefore of the

Liturgy and Reflection Questions for whichever chapter/story your group chooses to discuss.

3. The Weekly Convener will also share the Group Guidelines with the group each week as a reminder of the values and principles that guide their engagement and discussion together.

GROUP GUIDELINES

The Weekly Convener of the first gathering will begin by sharing the Group Guidelines. The Convener will hold space for group members to respond to the Group Guidelines, inviting clarifying questions and giving any additional guidance group members may need to feel seen and held in the group space. Weekly Conveners for subsequent gatherings will likewise begin by reading aloud the Group Guidelines and asking whether anyone has anything they need to add, signaling that these are living, breathing guidelines subject to change as needed for the safety of the whole.

1. Speak using "I" statements and from your own personal, lived experience.
2. When confused about something, become curious. Use phrases like, "Tell me more," and "I'd love to hear more about ________."
3. Don't assume you know what someone else is thinking or feeling. It's always best to ask them rather than to assume you know on their behalf.
4. What is said in the group stays in the group. This also means that what is said in the group is not to be discussed with others (including group members) outside of the group setting. And, from week to week, something said the week prior is only okay to reference if the person who said it says it again and invites reflection on it. In short, hold people's stories, comments, questions, and reflections with the utmost care, confidentiality, and discretion.
5. Release the need for certainty and instead embrace mystery. Practice saying, "I don't know" or "I'm still figuring out how I feel about that" when presented with a complex or difficult idea or question.

6. Allow room to breathe. Become comfortable with silence. Allow space after each person speaks.
7. When sharing a personal experience that contains sensitive and potentially activating content, offer a warning before sharing so that others in the group can make their own decision about whether they want to hear it or not.
8. Avoid cross talk and the impulse to try to "fix" someone else. We gather first to listen and then to respond. The main goal of being together is not to debate a particular topic or to fix one another; rather, it is to hold space for our stories, curiosities, and experiences to be spoken aloud. Even if you resonate deeply with what someone has shared or have a resource you are certain will help, resist the impulse to speak, and let the quiet speak for you.
9. Share by invitation, not demand. Listen to your own wisdom about when and what and how you need to speak (or not) into the circle.
10. Finally, be as present as possible. Silence your phone. Eliminate any other distractions. For the time the group gathers, commit to keeping your attention as undivided as your mind, body, and spirit allow.

GATHERING

Below is the format to use when gathering in your small group for liturgy, prayer, and reflection. The format works best when held no fewer than sixty minutes and no longer than eighty minutes.

1. CIRCLE: Group members gather in a circle. The Weekly Convener lights the candle in the middle of the circle.
2. LITURGY: Each gathering begins by practicing the liturgy from the chapter you'll be discussing during your time together. Though the liturgies are titled *morning*, *midday*, *evening*, and *night*, they can be practiced at any time of the day, whenever your group meets. The Weekly Convener will read the regular typeface lines from the liturgy, and group members will read the bold typeface lines. Allow fifteen to twenty minutes to practice and pray the liturgy together.

3. BODY BREAK: After the liturgy concludes, invite a five-minute body break for stretching, going to the bathroom, deep breathing, etc.
4. WEEKLY CHECK-IN: As the group reconvenes, invite a twelve-minute check-in asking each member to respond to the question: "What's the past week been like for you?" (Each person has two minutes to share, so invite comments that are short and to the point.)
5. DEEPER REFLECTION: For the next thirty to forty minutes, engage the "Deeper Reflection" questions at the end of the chapter you're discussing for the week. The Weekly Convener will ask the first question and hold space for group members to respond. The Group Guidelines are particularly important to remember and follow at this point. Group members will respond from their own experiences and will allow silence and space between each person's sharing. The Weekly Convener will determine when to move to the next question, and/or the group can decide together ahead of time which questions they want to discuss. There is no need to finish all the questions; engaging only one or two questions may be enough for the meeting. The Weekly Convener will pay attention to the time, and when the period of deeper reflection ends, the group will say these words together:
6. We honor both what has been said and what has remained unsaid in this sacred circle, and we hold one another's stories, lives, hearts, and beings with respect, gratitude, and love. Until next time, may the God of joy and justice, liturgy and love hold us, comfort us, and guide us to people and places we never thought we'd go. Amen.
7. PUBLIC WITNESS: Invite group members to share one way in which they will practice the liturgy in their daily lives in the week ahead (voting, giving money to a woman-centered organization, etc.) This should take approximately five minutes.
8. CLOSING: The Weekly Convener will decide how to close the circle by choosing one of the prayers from the week's liturgy, by saying *The Prayer of the Women*, or by using some other short

blessing to end the time together. After a closing blessing, the Weekly Convener will blow out the center candle, indicating that the small group gathering has concluded.

In the Beginning Were the Women Playlist

Scan the QR code using the camera on your smartphone, and it will take you to a public playlist on Spotify containing the songs included in the Contemporary Connection section of each chapter. Because you must have a Spotify account to access the playlist, you may also visit claireemckeeverburgett.com/music for links to YouTube videos of each song, as well as for a simple recording of me singing "In the Beginning" a cappella.

In the Beginning Were the Women Reading and Resource List

The following books and websites helped me write this book by providing insight, research, inspiration, and background to the women of the Hebrew Bible. I highly recommend that you read them for greater context and information, as well.

Sisters in the Wilderness: The Challenge of Womanist God by Delores S. Williams

Jewish Women's Archive[44]

[44] https://jwa.org/

Moses, Man of the Mountain by Zora Neale Hurston

Womanist Midrash by Wilda Gafney

Teaching to Transgress: Education as the Practice of Freedom by bell hooks

The Color Purple by Alice Walker

The Dance of the Dissident Daughter by Sue Monk Kidd

Midrash: Reading the Bible with Question Marks by Sandy Eisenberg Sasso

A Troubling in My Soul: Womanist Perspectives on Evil and Suffering, Emilie M. Townes, editor

The Red Tent by Anita Diamant

Beloved by Toni Morrison

Acknowledgments

There's no way this book would be in your hands if it weren't for the beautiful souls who came alongside me to help it be born.

To my publisher...thank you for believing in the work to center and celebrate women and for knowing another book about, by, for, and with women needed to be written.

To my editor, Ulrike Guthrie...thank you for making this book clearer, kinder, stronger, and truer at every turn.

To Devon and Amy...thank you for being my chosen sisters. Living this life with you makes life sweeter and easier. I love you.

To Beth Richardson...thank you for your willingness to take a voice recording of my song, turning into a real-live melody on a page that people other than me can sing. You're the best.

To Marjorie...thank you for your genuine guidance and prayerful presence in my life. You reflect to me who I truly am, which, in turn helps me be a more honest writer and human being. Thank you for continuing to come alongside me in all of the ebbs and flows of life.

To all of you who purchased, read, and shared *Blessed Are the Women*...thank you! Your support of my work helped make this book possible.

To Kent...thank you for walking the road of caretaking with me. Though you are miles away, I feel your presence with me, and I am grateful we are siblings and friends. Both help make the load feel a little bit lighter.

To Mom and Dad...when people ask me how I became who I am, I simply say, "I'm the daughter of Russell and Susan McKeever." At every turn, you've taught me what it means to be present, prayerful, loving, and kind. Thank you for being you, which, in turn, helps me be more me. I love you forever.

To Wade and Liv...for being mine and for being completely your own, thank you, and I love you. I'm with you. I believe in you.

I'm proud of you. No matter what. You are my whole heart and more. May you know the women, may you listen to the women, and may you follow the women forever.

Finally, to Adam…you read the first iterations of this book and gave me honest feedback every step of the way. Thank you—for being a trustworthy partner, lover, reader, co-parent, and friend. There's no one with whom I'd rather live this life than you. I love you. I thank you. Forever.

Biography

Claire K. McKeever-Burgett is an author, theologian, creative contemplative, and spiritual leader who has dedicated her life to bridging spirituality and social justice. With a background in English and Professional Writing from Baylor University and a Master of Divinity from Vanderbilt Divinity School, she has served as a clergy person, led congregations, and facilitated transformative writing, movement, and liturgical practices centered on healing and embodiment. A mother, communications professional, certified birth and postpartum doula, and a yoga, dance, and martial arts instructor, Claire lives with her family in Nashville, Tennessee. She writes regularly on Substack: *Blessed Are the Women (and other Good News for all of us)*.[45]

[45] https://clairemckeeverburgett.substack.com/